IN JESUS' TIME

TEACHING BIBLE HISTORY
TO CHILDREN . . .
OF ALL AGES

Kathryn L. Merrilll

and

Kristy L. Christian

Rainbow Books, Inc.

The authors gratefully acknowledge permission to use the following copyrighted material:

From *Anchor Bible*, Vols. 29 & 29A, eds. William Foxwell Albright and David Noel Freedman. Copyright 1970 by Doubleday, a division of Bantam, Doubleday, Dell Publishing Group, Inc. Used by permission.

From *Biblical Affirmations Of Woman* by Leonard Swidler, Westminster Press, Philadelphia, PA, 1979. Used by permission.

From *The Interpreter's Dictionary Of The Bible*, Vols. 3 & 4. Copyright renewal © 1990 by Abingdon Press. Used by permission.

From *Jesus And Woman* by Lisa Sergio. Copyright © 1975 by EPM Publications, Inc. Used by permission.

From *Living in the Time of Jesus of Nazareth* by Peter Connolly, Oxford University Press, London, 1983. Used by permission.

Reprinted by permission: *Getting Better Acquainted With Your Bible* by Berenice M. Shotwell, Shadwold Press, Kennebunkport, ME, 1972.

Reprinted by permission: *About The Gospels* by C. H. Dodd, Cambridge University Press, New York, 1950.

Reprinted by permission of the publishers and the Loeb Classical Library from Clement of Alexandria: *The Rich Man's Salvation*, translated by G. W. Butterworth, Cambridge, MA: Harvard University Press, 1982.

Reprinted by permission of the publishers and the Loeb Classical Library from Eusebius: *Ecclesiastical History*, Vol. I, translated by Kirsopp Lake, Cambridge, MA: Harvard University Press, 1980.

Reproduced from *Jesus And His Times,* copyright 1987, The Reader's Digest Association, Inc. Used by permission. Illustrator: Ray Skibinski.

IN JESUS' TIME
Teaching Bible History To Children . . . Of All Ages
by Kathryn L. Merrill and Kristy L. Christian
Copyright © 1993 by Kathryn L. Merrill and Kristy L. Christian
Cover Design by Marilyn Ratzlaff
Interior Design by Marilyn Ratzlaff
ISBN: 0-935834-93-1

Library of Congress Cataloging in Publication Data:
Kathryn L. Merrill, 1950-
  Teaching Bible history to children—of all ages / Kathryn L. Merrill & Kristy L. Christian.
    p.   cm.
  Includes bibliographical references.
  Contents: v. 1. In Jesus' time.
  ISBN 0-935834-93-1 (v. 1) : $16.95
  1. Bible—Study and teaching. 2. Bible—History of contemporary events. 3. Christian education of children. I. Christian, Kristy L., 1953- . II. Title.
BS600.2.M45   1993
220.0—dc20   92-34224
                                                                           CIP

This book is one of a series. Future books in this series will include:

- How the Bible Began
- The Patriarchs
- Moses and the Law
- David: From Shepherd Boy to King
- Letters to the Seven Churches in Asia
- Prophets & Prophecy
- Paul & Early Christianity
- Healings in the Bible
- Women in the Bible

*This book is dedicated to
B. Cobbey Crisler and Betty Ann Ridley,
whose undaunted love for the Bible
has touched the lives of so many and
encouraged all of us to live its inspired Word.*

CONTENTS

ACKNOWLEDGMENTS

Many thanks to our editors, Melissa G. Peterson and Kathleen W. Starrett. Thank you for working those long hours in order for this book to be the best it could be.

Many thanks to Marilyn Ratzlaff and Peggy Bryant. We are so grateful they didn't give up on us. And to Betty Wright — who kept the faith that this project would be finished some day.

PREFACE

To Parents, Teachers, and Bible Students:

Our goal in putting together a series of books on "Teaching Bible History to Children" is motivated by our desire to bring the Scriptures to life. Nothing can take the place of individual inspiration, prayer, and study. However, in order to realize the full scope of Christianity's influence on the world, a knowledge of Bible events in relation to their historical context (people, politics, geography, social customs, religious traditions, chronological events, etc.) is vital to give the student a foundation on which to build a deeper understanding of the Biblical text and its relevance to our lives today.

As sincere Bible students, can we only stay on the surface of the Scriptures? When we remember Jesus' admonition to "Search the Scriptures" (see John 5:39), aren't we impelled to explore more fully the deeper truths to be found there? Professor C. H. Dodd writes about the Gospel of John, ". . . John insists that we shall pause over every single incident as we go through the story, until we have got below the surface and seen what it means" (*About the Gospels*, p. 43).

Our hope is that this course of study will serve as a springboard to launch the student into a lifetime of Biblical discovery!

Sincerely,

Kristy L. Christian

Kristy L. Christian

Kathryn L. Merrill

Kathryn L. Merrill

INTRODUCTORY ACTIVITIES

CONTENTS:

- Basic Structure of Lesson Packets
- Master Schedule
- Pretest
- How to Use a Bible Concordance
- Reading a Gospel
- Family Life in Jesus' Time

MATERIALS:

- Bible Dictionary
- Bible & Concordance
- Reader's Digest, *Jesus and His Times*
- Activity Sheets

MEMORY VERSE:

"In the beginning was the Word, and the Word was with God, and the Word was God."

John 1:1

BASIC STRUCTURE OF THE LESSON PACKETS

Each Lesson Packet will include the following information:
- Activity Sheets*
- Teacher's Notes
- Materials Needed to Complete the Lesson
- Directions for the Teacher or Parent
- Extended Study Topics (not in all Lesson Packets)

Each Lesson Packet may be studied separately, though every packet builds upon the preceding one. The Master Schedule offers a suggested course outline which can be adapted to one's individual or group needs. A Glossary of terms and names is located at the back of the book for reference.

MEMORY VERSE

A Bible verse for memorization is found on the first page of each Lesson Packet.

---

*The Activity Sheets found in this book are available in separate packets from the publisher.

MASTER SCHEDULE

To simplify the voluminous material on this subject, a calendar of each day's outline is presented as a guideline for individual or group study. The calendar is divided into a minimum of 20 one-hour units or lessons. This leaves the flexibility to focus on any particular topic that may interest the students for a longer period of time.

The Master Schedule sets up a sequential study — each lesson building on the one preceding it. Writing the answers on paper is helpful because it reinforces what the student hears or reads; however, with younger children who cannot read or write, the Lesson Packets can be adapted to make an oral presentation.

In addition to the Bible history lessons, it is recommended that one of the Gospels be read simultaneously. The Gospel of Mark is thought to be the first Gospel written, and it is the shortest (16 chapters). In the case of younger children, the parent and the child should take turns reading aloud one-on-one. Use the chart on page 18 to organize some "on the surface" themes.

We recommend watching the video , " Jesus of Nazareth" at the end of the final Lesson Packet.

1	2	3	4	5
Pretest; How to Use a Bible Concordance	Map of Israel Start Gospel Reading	People Other Than Disciples	Disciple & Apostle Charts	Disciple & Apostle Charts
6	**7**	**8**	**9**	**10**
Time Line Gospel Reading	Bible Vocabulary English Terms	Bible Vocabulary Greek Words	Jesus' Three-Year Ministry	Jesus as Healer
11	**12**	**13**	**14**	**15**
Jesus' Treatment of Women Gospel Reading	Jesus as Teacher	Jesus as Prophet	The Temple and Jewish Religious Worship	The Temple and Jewish Religious Worship
16	**17**	**18**	**19**	**20**
Crucifixion Gospel Reading	PASSION WEEK — Resurrection — Appearances		Review of Material	Bible Test; Map Test; Retake the Pretest

13

INTRODUCTORY ACTIVITIES
PRETEST
What Do I Already Know?

Before starting this unit, "In Jesus' Time," take ten minutes and answer the following questions. Keep the paper, and after you have read through all of the historical material, take the pretest again and see how much you have learned. If you are doing this with a Sunday School class, have them do the same exercise.

1. PEOPLE IN THE GOSPELS

Whom do you know? _____

_____

_____

2. PLACES IN THE GOSPELS

Name all the places that you know.

_____

_____

3. GOVERNMENT

Who governed Palestine in Jesus' time?

_____

_____

4. HEALINGS OF JESUS

List all the healings you remember from the Gospels.

_____

_____

5. TEACHINGS OF JESUS

What teachings by Jesus do you know?

_____

_____

_____

6. GOSPELS

Name the Gospels and who wrote them.

_____

_____

_____

7. DISCIPLES

Name the twelve disciples.

_____

_____

8. DATES

When did Jesus live?

_____

9. JEWISH CELEBRATIONS

Describe the many Jewish celebrations in first-century Palestine.

_____

_____

_____

INTRODUCTORY ACTIVITIES
HOW TO USE A BIBLE CONCORDANCE

Directions: This exercise is for twelve-year-olds and up. The first two assignments are samples using Strong's *Exhaustive Bible Concordance.*

Assignment 1 — Look up the word "disciple," find one instruction Jesus gives to his disciples.

Step 1: Look up the word *disciple* in Strong's.

Step 2: In that list find a verse (in the Gospels) where *Jesus said unto his disciples . . .*

Step 3: Example: Matt. 16:24. *"Said Jesus unto his d., if any man . . ."* Look up the verse in the Bible and write down the instruction.

Assignment 2 — Find the original Greek meaning of the word *disciple.*

Step 1: Look up the word *disciple* in Strong's. Find in the right hand column a number.

Step 2: Word *disciple* is #3101 in the Greek Dictionary found in back of Strong's *Exhaustive Bible Concordance* (on page 45 of the Dictionary).

Step 3: The word is *mathetes* — which means a learner, pupil, disciple. (The word "mathematics" comes from this Greek word.)

INTRODUCTORY ACTIVITIES
CONCORDANCE PRACTICE ACTIVITIES

BIBLE MESSENGERS

Directions: Use a Bible concordance to find out who brought the news to each of these people about Jesus:

1. Shepherds in the field
2. Mary of Nazareth
3. Simon Peter
4. Publicans and soldiers
5. Herod the Great
6. an Ethiopian
7. Nathanael

BIBLE OCCUPATIONS

Directions: Use a Bible concordance to find the answers and match the occupation with the Bible character:

1. _____Luke   a. tentmaker
2. _____Matthew   b. Roman governor
3. _____Caiaphas   c. fisherman
4. _____Paul   d. physician
5. _____Pilate   e. tax collector
6. _____Zacchaeus   f. publican
7. _____Peter   g. high priest
8. _____Herod   h. king
9. _____Cornelius   i. centurion

Answers:
1. *Luke 2:8-11*, angel of the Lord
2 *Luke 1:26*, angel Gabriel
3. *John 1:40-41*, Andrew, his brother
4. *Luke 3:12-16*, John the Baptist
5. *Matt. 2:1-4*, wise men
6. *Acts 8:26-27*, Philip the Evangelist
7. *John 1:45*, Philip the disciple

Answers:
1. d
2. e
3. g
4. a
5. b
6. f
7. c
8. h
9. i

INTRODUCTORY ACTIVITIES
READING A GOSPEL

Directions: Choose one of the four Gospels to read aloud with your child. Use the chart to organize in thought some "on the surface" themes. Study the Gospel chapter by chapter. Look for healings, particular teachings, names of people, places, major events in Jesus' life, and any vocabulary words you don't know. Use one chart for every chapter in a Gospel. This is a good activity for students and parents to share together.

GOSPEL _____	Chapter and Verse		Chapter and Verse
Healings:		Teachings:	
People:		Places:	
Specific events:		Words I don't know:	
Verses where the author quotes from Old Testament passages:		Other themes:	

INTRODUCTORY ACTIVITIES
FAMILY LIFE IN JESUS' TIME

Directions: Research and answer the following questions.
(Answers on pages 20-21)

1. What kind of houses did people live in?_____

   _____

2. How did people light their houses? _____

   _____

3. Where did they find water? _____

   _____

4. What did the people eat and drink? _____

   _____

5. What clothing was available? _____

   _____

6. What was the mode of transportation during Jesus' time? _____

   _____

7. Name the language(s) spoken by those living in Palestine? _____

   _____

8. How did children study and learn? _____

   _____

9. Who ruled the country during the time of Jesus? _____

   _____

INTRODUCTORY ACTIVITIES
FAMILY LIFE IN JESUS' TIME

Answers to Family Life in Jesus' Time research questions. More in-depth answers may be found in the Reader's Digest, *Jesus and His Times*, and *Handbook of Life in Bible Times* by J. A. Thompson.

1. Houses were usually packed closely together because space was limited in many areas. Most people lived in one-story houses with flat roofs. Only the wealthy lived in houses with several rooms. The rooftop was called the "upper room," and it was used for cooking, sleeping, and entertaining. Sometimes religious ceremonies were conducted there. Houses were made of dried brick or rough stone. Floors were made of clay. In wealthier houses, floors were sometimes paved. Roofs were made of branches which were woven together and then covered with clay. There were no bathrooms. Washing was done in the street or courtyard. Animals were cared for in the houses, but kept below the living area.

     Jesus had to leave the towns or villages and retire to the wilderness or garden to find quiet.

2. Houses were lit by clay lamps which burned coarse olive oil or fat. The light usually lasted two to four hours.

3. Water was scarce in Palestine. Wells were dug below the surface to reach the water supply. Other sources of water were the springs in and around the towns. Also, cisterns were built to catch rain water.

4. Sheep and goats were kept for milk, cheese, meat, and wool. Chickens were raised for meat and eggs. Bread was baked in a large oven kept outside in the courtyard. Other available foods were melons, figs, vegetables, nuts, wild fowl, and fish. Pork was forbidden. Wild honey or date syrups sweetened their foods. Families ate with their fingers by dipping bread in bowls.

5. Both men and women wore tunics. Men's tunics were tied with leather belts or cloth girdles. Men wore sandals and sometimes wore a white cloth over their heads. Most women wore head coverings and sandals, too. In public, women covered their faces with a veil.

INTRODUCTORY ACTIVITIES
FAMILY LIFE IN JESUS' TIME (Cont.)

6. Transportation in Palestine was either by foot, donkey, camel, or boat. Wealthy people used carriages, a two-wheeled cart or four-wheeled wagon. Litters were also used by the wealthy. Six or eight bearers balanced them on their shoulders. Caravans were available to join, if one was traveling a long distance.

7. Aramaic, Hebrew, Greek, and Latin were spoken.

8. Only boys went to school. They learned to read and write. In the synagogue, boys were taught the Old Testament by a rabbi. Education consisted entirely of the Torah (written law) and the traditions handed down by spiritual teachers through the centuries. Girls were taught by their mothers whatever they needed to know to fulfill their obligations as wives and mothers according to Jewish tradition. Girls were not taught the Scriptures.

9. Rome. At the time of Jesus' birth, Herod the Great was in power. Pontius Pilate, as a Roman procurator or governor, ruled during the adult life of Jesus. The Jews had a supreme court called the Sanhedrin which made decisions regarding Jewish life.

GEOGRAPHY IN JESUS' TIME

CONTENTS:

- **Filled-in Map and Directions**
- **Blank Map**
- **Geography Charts**

MATERIALS:

- **Bible Dictionary**
- **Bible Atlas for further study**

MEMORY VERSE:

". . . Suffer the little children to come unto me . . . for of such is the kingdom of God."

Mark 10:14

GEOGRAPHY IN JESUS' TIME
PALESTINE IN THE TIME OF JESUS

Directions: Looking at the "filled-in" map, talk about places the students have heard of and include the events that occurred there. Using the "blank" map, ask the students to identify the places they can remember. Use a highlighter to accent certain locations. Children also enjoy coloring the map. Hang it up and use it often as a resource.

Every time you come together with the students, see how many places they can locate. Do it over and over again until the cities, rivers, and regions are firmly fixed in thought. Another activity is for the students to look up these places in a Bible concordance and see if or where they are mentioned in the Bible.

More background information about the places located on the map may be found in the Teacher's Notes at the back of this Lesson Packet.

PLACES ON THE MAP

Bethany	Gaza	Mt. Gerizim
Bethlehem	Gergesa	Mt. Hermon
Bethsaida	Idumaea *	Nain
Caesarea Maritima	Jericho	Nazareth
Caesarea Philippi	Jerusalem	Peraea *
Capernaum	Joppa	Samaria *
Cana	Jordan River	Samaria
Damascus	Judaea *	Sea of Galilee
Dead Sea	Lydda	Sepphoris
Decapolis *	Magdala	Shechem
Emmaus	Masada	Sidon
Gadara	Mediterranean Sea	Sychar
Galilee *	Mt. Carmel	Tyre

* Territories

GEOGRAPHY IN JESUS' TIME
PALESTINE IN THE TIME OF JESUS
(Filled-In)

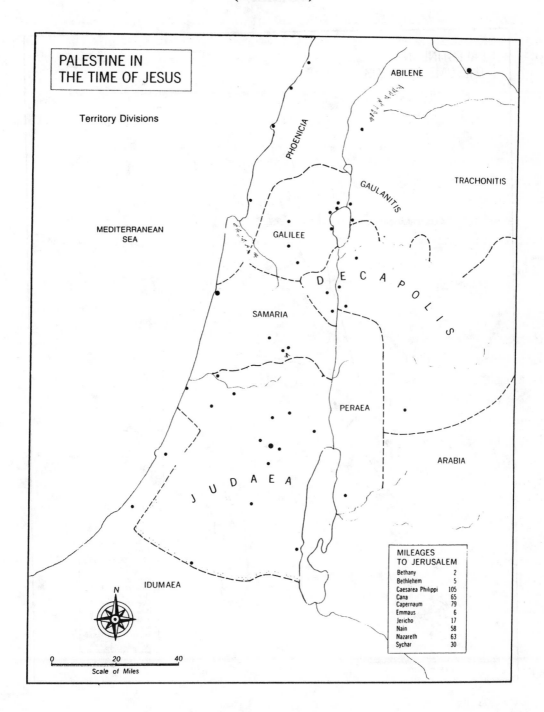

PALESTINE IN
THE TIME OF JESUS

Territory Divisions

ABILENE

PHOENICIA

TRACHONITIS

GAULANITIS

MEDITERRANEAN
SEA

GALILEE

D E C A P O L I S

SAMARIA

PERAEA

ARABIA

J U D A E A

N

IDUMAEA

MILEAGES TO JERUSALEM	
Bethany	2
Bethlehem	5
Caesarea Philippi	105
Cana	65
Capernaum	79
Emmaus	6
Jericho	17
Nain	58
Nazareth	63
Sychar	30

0   20   40
Scale of Miles

GEOGRAPHY IN JESUS' TIME
PALESTINE IN THE TIME OF JESUS
(Blank)

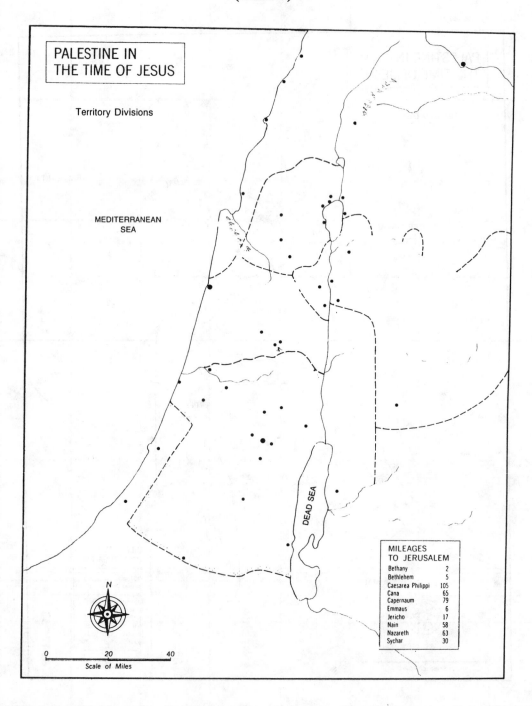

PALESTINE IN
THE TIME OF JESUS

Territory Divisions

MEDITERRANEAN
SEA

DEAD SEA

MILEAGES
TO JERUSALEM

Bethany	2
Bethlehem	5
Caesarea Philippi	105
Cana	65
Capernaum	79
Emmaus	6
Jericho	17
Nain	58
Nazareth	63
Sychar	30

N

0   20   40
Scale of Miles

FAMOUS BIBLE PLACES	LOCATION	EVENTS	HEALINGS	PEOPLE	INTERESTING FACTS
Jerusalem					
Capernaum					
Bethany					
Bethsaida					
Nazareth					
Jericho					
Caesarea Philippi					

FAMOUS BIBLE PLACES	LOCATION	EVENTS	HEALINGS	PEOPLE	INTERESTING FACTS
Bethlehem					
Samaria					
Caesarea Maritima					
Masada					
Herodium*					
Praetorium*					
Jordan River					

*To be researched by the student

FAMOUS BIBLE PLACES	LOCATION	EVENTS	HEALINGS	PEOPLE	INTERESTING FACTS
Gethsemane and Mt. of Olives					
Qumran					
Cana					
Emmaus					
Sea of Galilee					
Mt. Tabor					
Decapolis					

GEOGRAPHY IN JESUS' TIME
BACKGROUND INFORMATION

Bethany (*"house of dates"*)
Located 1.7 miles from Jerusalem; home of Mary, Martha, and Lazarus (John 11:1); Jesus often stayed here — it was his home in Judaea (Matt. 21:17); Jesus raised Lazarus from the dead (John 11:1-44); Jesus was in the home of Simon the leper (Mark 14:3-9); the site of Jesus' ascension (Luke 24:50-51).

Bethlehem (*"house of bread"*)
Located 6 miles south of Jerusalem, near the major north-south route linking Jerusalem with Hebron and the Negev Desert; the prophet Micah foretold of Jesus' birth (Mic. 5:2; Matt. 2:4-6); shepherds visited the infant Jesus (Luke 2:8-20); the wise men also visited the infant (Matt. 2:1-12); Herod had the children killed (Matt. 2:13-23); Joseph came here to pay his taxes.

Bethsaida (*"place of nets"*)
Located on the east side of the Jordan River about 1 1/2 miles north of the point where the Jordan River enters the Sea of Galilee; birthplace of Peter, Andrew, and Philip (John 1:44; 12:21); some scholars believe the feeding of the 5,000 and the 4,000 was near here (Matt. 14:13-21; 15:32-38); the blind man was healed after Jesus led him out of the town (Mark 8:22-26); the town does not exist today.

Caesarea Maritima (*named in honor of Caesar Augustus — Luke 2:1*)
Located as a seaport on the Mediterranean Sea, 70 miles northwest of Jerusalem; built by Herod the Great in 22 B.C. as his summer palace; capital of the Roman government in Palestine for 500 years; home of Pontius Pilate. Here many Jews and Christians were thrown to the lions after the revolt in A.D. 66; the Christian scholar Origen established the School of Caesarea; Eusebius was bishop of Caesarea from A.D. 313-340; Peter preached to Cornelius (Acts 10); Paul spent two years in prison (Acts 23:22-26, 33).

Capernaum (*"town of Nahum"*)
Located about 2 1/2 miles from where the Jordan River enters the Sea of Galilee. A customs station; also apparently a Roman military post along a highway which ran from Damascus to Galilee and south to Jerusalem; the center of Jesus' activities for 18-20 months — more healings and miracles

GEOGRAPHY IN JESUS' TIME
BACKGROUND INFORMATION (Cont.)

occurred here than in any other city; one of the finest ruins of a synagogue excavated here; Jesus called Peter, Andrew, James, John, and Matthew to be disciples (Matt. 4:13, 18-22); Peter lived here (Matt. 8:5, 14); Jesus taught in the synagogue (Mark 1:21).

Cana *("place of reeds")*
Tradition locates the town a short distance northeast of Nazareth; home of the disciple Nathanael (John 21:2); site of Jesus' first miracle — changing water into wine at the wedding feast (John 2:1-11); while in Cana, Jesus healed a nobleman's son who lived in Capernaum (John 4:46-54).

Damascus
Located 140 miles northeast of Jerusalem; Paul recovered his sight here (Acts 9:10-18).

Dead Sea
47 miles long, 10 miles wide, 1,292 feet below sea level — the lowest region on the earth's surface; salt lake which has no outlet; Jordan River flows into it; no marine life can exist in its waters; Dead Sea scrolls discovered near the Dead Sea and Qumran.

Decapolis *(ten cities)*
A federation of Greek cities in Palestine (Matt. 4:25) founded to protect themselves, the trade routes, and the interests of Rome.

Emmaus *(comes from word Hamma, which means "warm well")*
Bible scholars have not been able to confirm the location of this site; some say 7 miles northwest of Jerusalem, others calculate the distance at 20 miles. According to Luke, the site of Emmaus is where Jesus appeared to two disciples on the evening of his resurrection (Luke 24:13).

Gadara *(area of the Gadarenes)*
Located 5 to 6 miles southeast of the Sea of Galilee; a city of Decapolis; some scholars believe that the actual site of the demoniac healing (Matt. 8:28-34) was **Gergesa** on the upper east bank of the Sea of Galilee.

GEOGRAPHY IN JESUS' TIME
BACKGROUND INFORMATION (Cont.)

Galilee *("the circle") (territory)*
Northern area of Palestine in the days of Jesus; 60 miles long, 30 miles wide; Jesus spent most of his life here; eleven disciples were Galileans; the territory encompassed 204 towns, including Aramaean, Phoenician, Greek, and Jewish (Matt. 4:12-25).

Gaza *("the strong place")*
A Philistine city located 3 miles from the Mediterranean Sea in the territory of Idumaea; land gateway between Egypt and Asia for caravan and military traffic; Philip went towards Gaza and on the way he met and baptized the Ethiopian eunuch (Acts 8:26-27).

Idumaea *(territory)*
Region south of Judaea occupied by Edomite refugees; Herod the Great was an Idumaean.

Jericho *("city of palm trees")*
Located 5 miles west of the Jordan River, 6 miles north of the Dead Sea, 17 miles northeast of Jerusalem; a stone tower excavated here dating 8,000 years old — the oldest building on earth; Zacchaeus was converted (Luke 19:1-27); great multitudes followed Jesus in Jericho (Matt. 20:29); Jesus cured Bartimaeus and his companion (Mark 10:46-52).

Jerusalem
Located 38 miles east of the Mediterranean Sea and 14 miles west of the Dead Sea; Rome besieged the city in 63 B.C. More wars were fought here than any other city in the world. The great Temple of Herod was built here for the Jews — begun in 20 B.C. and completed in A.D. 64. The city was destroyed in A.D. 70. Mary came to Jerusalem to offer a sacrifice according to the law after Jesus' birth (Luke 2:22); Jesus visited the Temple at age 12 (Luke 2:41-50); Jesus cleansed the Temple (John 2:12-25; Matt. 21:12-16); Jesus healed the blind and lame; taught here.

Joppa
Located 35 miles northwest of Jerusalem; 8,000 Jews killed at Joppa under

GEOGRAPHY IN JESUS' TIME
BACKGROUND INFORMATION (Cont.)

the Romans. During the crusades, 20,000 Christians were slain here. Peter raised Dorcas from the dead (Acts 9:36-42).

Jordan River
200 miles long between the Sea of Galilee and the Dead Sea, but its distance covers only 65 miles in a straight line; most of its course flows below sea level. Mt. Hermon is its source. John the Baptist came out of the wilderness to preach the coming of the kingdom of heaven; Jesus was baptized here (Mark 1:4-11).

Judaea *(territory)*
Its region is the southern part of western Palestine. Jerusalem is located in this area; formerly the area of the tribe of Judah.

Lydda *(Lod)*
Located 11 miles southeast of Joppa; Greeks changed the name of Lod to Lydda; Jewish exiles settled here after the Babylonian captivity; Peter healed Aeneas (Acts 9:32-35).

Magdala
Located on the western shore of the Galilean Sea; fishing industry flourished here; home of Mary Magdalene (Luke 8:2); Jesus came here after feeding the 4,000 (Matt. 15:39).

Masada
Located 2 1/2 miles from the western shore of the Dead Sea in the wilderness of Judaea; it is 2,000 feet above sea level. Herod the Great built his winter palace here; scene of the last stand of the Jewish revolt against the Romans which began in A.D. 66; some 906 people committed suicide leaving the Romans nothing to take.

Mediterranean Sea
Inland ocean extending about 2,200 miles. Ship traffic during New Testament times made Paul's missionary activity possible.

GEOGRAPHY IN JESUS' TIME
BACKGROUND INFORMATION (Cont.)

Mt. Carmel
Mountain range 13 miles long projecting into the Mediterranean Sea; its highest point is 1,810 feet above sea level.

Mt. Gerizim
Stands 2,900 feet above sea level; held sacred by the Samaritans; a Samaritan temple was built here; Jacob's well is at the foot of the mount; Jesus spoke to the Samaritan woman about true worship (John 4:4-30).

Nain
A town of southwest Galilee — 5 miles southeast of Nazareth; Jesus raised the widow's son near the gate of the town (Luke 7:11-17).

Nazareth
Located 15 miles southeast of the Sea of Galilee; 20 miles from the Mediterranean Sea; home of Joseph and Mary (Luke 1:26); the angel came to Mary and Joseph here (Luke 1:26-38); Jesus lived here with his parents as a boy (Luke 2:39, 51); an insignificant town according to the disciple Nathanael (John 1:46); Jesus read from the book of Isaiah in a synagogue; the crowd then attempted to throw him from the brow of the hill (Luke 4:16-30).

Peraea *(territory)*
Region bounded on the west by the Jordan River and the northeast portion of the Dead Sea; Jesus and his disciples came into this area after they left Galilee for the last time. Significant as the route Jesus took on his way to Jerusalem.

Samaria *(territory)*
Extremely productive agricultural area; over the centuries the region has been subject to many invaders and conquerors; territory given to Herod the Great in 30 B.C., then bequeathed to his son, who lost it in A.D. 6; after that Roman procurators controlled it. Jews during Jesus' time mainly avoided the area in traveling to Judaea because Jews had no dealings with the Samaritans, however, Jesus traveled through the area (Luke 17:11; John 4:4).

GEOGRAPHY IN JESUS' TIME
BACKGROUND INFORMATION (Cont.)

Samaria (city — "watch")
Located 42 miles north of Jerusalem; capital of the northern kingdom and burial place of the kings of Israel. Its inhabitants, along with the Ten Tribes of Israel, were taken captive in 772 B.C. and lost to history. Those who remained in the area, intermarried with the captives brought from the conquered countries, and descendants from these mixed marriages were called Samaritans. Jews shunned Samaritans because of the intermarriages.

Sea of Galilee
Heart-shaped body of water; 696 feet below sea level; about 12 miles long, 5-6 miles wide, 200 feet deep; in New Testament times, known as Gennesaret (Luke 5:1); also named Tiberias; several cities along its northwest shoreline. Because of the height of the mountains surrounding it, the area is subject to sudden and violent storms. Jesus called his disciples — Peter, Andrew, James, and others (Matt. 4:18-22); he spoke to the multitudes from Peter's boat (Mark 3:7-12); Jesus stilled the storm (Matt. 8-23-27); Jesus walked over the waves (Mark 6:45-52); Jesus healed and taught in and around the lake. He appeared to his disciples after the resurrection and prepared a morning meal for them by the shore (John 21:1-23).

Sepphoris ("birds")
Located 4 miles north of Nazareth; capital of Galilee in Jesus' youth. A New Testament professor suggests the possibility that Joseph and Jesus may have worked on the rebuilding of Sepphoris started by Herod Antipas.

Shechem (Nablus)
Located 40 miles north of Jerusalem; home to about 250 Samaritans. The Samaritan temple on Mt. Gerizim (which rises above the town) no longer exists, but Samaritans still celebrate Passover on Mt. Gerizim every year.

Sidon
Located 25 miles north of Tyre on the Mediterranean sea coast (in Lebanon); conquered by various world powers; men from Sidon heard Jesus (Mark 3:8). Jesus healed the daughter of a Syrophenician woman near here (Mark 7:24-30). Paul stopped here on his way to Rome (Acts 27:3).

GEOGRAPHY IN JESUS' TIME
BACKGROUND INFORMATION (Cont.)

Sychar
A city of Samaria; Jacob's well located here; Jesus talked to the Samaritan woman here (John 4:3-42).

Tyre
Located on a small island which was originally unconnected with the mainland; located 25 miles south of Sidon; people of Tyre heard Jesus preach (Luke 6:17); in the time of Paul, Christians lived here, and Paul visited them on his journey to Jerusalem.

Sources: *The Interpreter's Dictionary of the Bible* and *Where Jesus Walked.*

PEOPLE IN THE NEW TESTAMENT

CONTENTS:

- Fill-in-the-Blank Biographical Sketch
- Flash Cards
- Crossword Puzzle

MATERIALS:

- Bible Dictionary
- Bible & Concordance
- Glossary (Page 253)
- Two sets of Flash Cards per student
- Blank Bio List
- Scissors

MEMORY VERSE:

"Be ye therefore perfect, even as your Father which is in heaven is perfect."

Matthew 5:48

People in the New Testament
BIOGRAPHICAL SKETCH

Directions: Use the Glossary on page 253 or a Bible dictionary to describe these people and why they were important. For older students, look in a Bible concordance and find a Bible verse (when possible) to correspond with the name.

1. Anna _____

   _____

2. Caiaphas _____

   _____

3. Caesar Augustus _____

   _____

4. Cleopas _____

   _____

5. Elisabeth _____

   _____

6. Herod Agrippa I _____

   _____

7. Herod Antipater _____

   _____

8. Herod Archelaus _____

   _____

9. Herod the Great _____

   _____

People in the New Testament
BIOGRAPHICAL SKETCH (Cont.)

10. Herodias _____

_____

11. Jairus _____

_____

12. Joanna (wife of Chuza) _____

_____

13. John the Baptist _____

_____

14. Joseph (Mary's husband) _____

_____

15. Joseph of Arimathaea _____

_____

16. Lazarus _____

_____

17. Mary (Jesus' mother) _____

_____

18. Mary Magdalene _____

_____

19. Mary and Martha _____

_____

People in the New Testament
BIOGRAPHICAL SKETCH (Cont.)

20. Nicodemus _____

_____

21. Pompey _____

_____

22. Pontius Pilate _____

_____

23. Salome _____

_____

24. Simeon _____

_____

25. Simon the Pharisee _____

_____

26. Tiberius Caesar _____

_____

27. Zacchaeus _____

_____

28. Zacharias _____

_____

People in the New Testament
FLASH CARDS

FLASH CARD GAME WITH A PARTNER
Directions: Print the following names and words on flash cards and make one set with the name on one side and the answer on the back. Practice with a partner. One partner flashes the name while the other one says the answer out loud.

FLASH CARD GAME FOR ONE PERSON
Directions: Make two sets of flash cards — one set with all the names on one side and another set with all the definitions. Leave the back of each card blank. Put all the names on the left side and let the student match each name to a definition.

EXAMPLES

CAIAPHAS	**HIGH PRIEST IN SANHEDRIN**
JAIRUS	**RULER OF SYNAGOGUE WHOSE DAUGHTER JESUS RAISED FROM THE DEAD**

HEROD ANTIPATER	HEROD THE GREAT	HEROD ARCHELAUS
HEROD AGRIPPA I	ELISABETH	ZACHARIAS
JOHN THE BAPTIST	MARY (JESUS' MOTHER)	JOSEPH (HUSBAND OF MARY)
JAIRUS	MARY MAGDALENE	MARY & MARTHA
CLEOPAS	LAZARUS	NICODEMUS
CAIAPHAS	SIMON (THE PHARISEE)	JOSEPH OF ARIMATHAEA
JOANNA (WIFE OF CHUZA)	PONTIUS PILATE	ZACCHAEUS

RULER OF SYNAGOGUE WHOSE DAUGHTER JESUS RAISED FROM THE DEAD	HIGH PRIEST IN SANHEDRIN	FATHER OF HEROD THE GREAT
JESUS BORN DURING HIS REIGN; REBUILT THE TEMPLE	SON OF HEROD THE GREAT	RULER WHO KILLED THE DISCIPLE JAMES
MOTHER OF JOHN THE BAPTIST	FATHER OF JOHN THE BAPTIST	MOTHER OF JESUS
PREACHED IN THE WILDERNESS; BAPTIZED JESUS IN JORDAN RIVER	TOOK HIS FAMILY TO EGYPT TO SAFETY	MEMBER OF SANHEDRIN WHO VISITED JESUS BY NIGHT
MAN WHO OWNED THE TOMB WHERE THEY TOOK THE BODY OF JESUS	ROMAN GOVERNOR OF JUDAEA WHO AGREED TO CRUCIFY JESUS	A TAX COLLECTOR OF JERICHO WHOSE LIFE WAS TRANS-FORMED BY CONTACT WITH JESUS
HIS HOUSE IS WHERE JESUS WAS ANOINTED BY A SINFUL WOMAN	WIFE OF HEROD ANTIPAS' STEWARD — BELIEVED TO BE A FOLLOWER OF JESUS; WAS PRESENT AT THE EMPTY TOMB	PROMINENT WOMAN OF GALILEE WHO FOLLOWED JESUS; HE CAST OUT OF HER SEVEN DEMONS
JESUS RAISED HIM FROM THE DEAD IN BETHANY	ONE OF THE TWO DISCIPLES WHOM JESUS MET ON THE ROAD TO EMMAUS	SISTERS OF LAZARUS WHO LIVED IN BETHANY; JESUS OFTEN VISITED THEIR HOME

People in the New Testament
CROSSWORD PUZZLE

ACROSS CLUES:

1. Killed the male babies in Bethlehem
7. Father of John the Baptist
9. A Pharisee, with whom Jesus ate a meal
10. Husband of Mary
15. Climbed a tree to see Jesus
16. Came by night to talk to Jesus
17. A tax collector who became a disciple
18. A disciple who doubted Jesus

DOWN CLUES:

2. Mother of John the Baptist
3. Raised from the dead by Jesus after four days in a tomb
4. Baptized Jesus and others in the Jordan River
5. Mother of Jesus
6. Came to Jesus to heal his twelve-year-old daughter
8. Wife of Chuza, Herod's steward
11. Roman procurator, condemned Jesus to be crucified
12. Traitor to Jesus, turned him in to the Jewish authorities
13. Leader of the twelve disciples
14. High priest in the Sanhedrin

WORD LIST — BIBLE PEOPLE:

Caiaphas	Joanna	Peter
Elisabeth	Judas	Pilate
Herod	Lazarus	Simon
Jairus	Matthew	Thomas
Joseph	Mary	Zacchaeus
John	Nicodemus	Zacharias

People in the New Testament
CROSSWORD PUZZLE (Cont.)

Copyright © 1993 by Kristy L. Christian & Kathryn L. Merrill

ANSWERS:

DISCIPLES AND APOSTLES

CONTENTS:

- **How to Memorize the Disciples' Names**
- **Disciple/Apostle Charts**
- **Roman World Map**
- **Qualities of Disciple**
- **Origin of Gospels**
- **Comparison of Gospels**
- **Synopsis of Disciples/ Apostles**

MATERIALS:

- **Blank Charts**
- **Roman World Map**

MEMORY VERSE:

". . . If ye continue in my word, then are ye my disciples indeed; And ye shall know the truth, and the truth shall make you free."

John 8:31-32

DISCIPLES AND APOSTLES
HOW TO MEMORIZE THE DISCIPLES' NAMES

Practice memorizing the names of Jesus' twelve disciples. Here's how: Remember **52 PANT MAT!**

5 = 5 J's
1. James — brother of John
2. John
3. James — son of Alphaeus
4. Judas — also called Jude (Thaddaeus)
5. Judas Iscariot

2 = 2 S's
6. Simon the Zealot
7. Simon Peter

8. **P** = Philip
9. **A** = Andrew
10. **N** = Nathanael (Bartholomew)
11. **T** = Thomas

12. **MAT** = Matthew

CHARTS

Directions: Together with the students, write the answers in the Disciple and Apostle Charts using the Teacher's Notes at the end of this Lesson Packet. Talk about the answers as you go along. If you are unsure about any information, do not hesitate to look up the disciples' names yourself.

Resources for additional information:
Bible dictionaries: *Harper's, Smith's, Hastings, The Interpreter's Dictionary of the Bible,* Vols.1-4, *The Anchor Bible* series on the Gospels, Vols. 26-29.

DISCIPLE	OCCUPATION	ORIGINAL HOME	HOW WAS HE "CALLED"	BOOKS WRITTEN BY HIM	TRAVELS? WHERE DID HE PREACH?	WHAT HAPPENED IN THE END?	MISCELLANEOUS INFORMATION
Simon Peter							
John							
Andrew							
Thomas							
Matthew							
Judas Iscariot							

DISCIPLE	OCCUPATION	ORIGINAL HOME	HOW WAS HE "CALLED"	BOOKS WRITTEN BY HIM	TRAVELS? WHERE DID HE PREACH?	WHAT HAPPENED IN THE END?	MISCELLANEOUS INFORMATION
Philip							
Simon the Zealot							
James, Brother of John							
Nathanael or Bartholomew							
James, Son of Alphaeus							
Judas or Thaddaeus							

50

APOSTLE	OCCUPATION	ORIGINAL HOME	HOW WAS HE "CALLED"	BOOKS WRITTEN BY HIM	TRAVELS? WHERE DID HE PREACH?	WHAT HAPPENED IN THE END?	MISCELLANEOUS INFORMATION
John Mark							
Luke							
Paul							
James, Brother of Jesus							
Stephen							

DISCIPLES AND APOSTLES
MAP OF THE ROMAN WORLD

Directions: Use the map of the Roman world to designate where tradition says some of the disciples ended up.

Roman World Of The First Century

Resource for additional information: Eusebius, *Ecclesiastical History*, Vol. I.

DISCIPLES AND APOSTLES
QUALITIES OF DISCIPLESHIP

Directions: What are the qualities that help us become disciples of Jesus Christ? What can we accomplish as his followers? These qualities can be determined by studying Jesus' treatment of individuals, Jesus' teachings, and Jesus' example.

The list is infinite, but below are a few verses to help one begin his study. Look up each verse and write it out.* On a separate sheet in your own words, write a paragraph on what it means to be a disciple. Describe what the world would be like if mankind lived these qualities on a daily basis.

* Summarize the quality in the column provided.

BIBLE VERSE	QUALITY
Matt. 6:33	
Matt. 6:25, 31, 34	
Matt. 10:42	
Matt. 18:2-3	

DISCIPLES AND APOSTLES
QUALITIES OF DISCIPLESHIP (Cont.)

BIBLE VERSE	QUALITY
John 14:27; Luke 8:50, 12:32; Matt. 14:27	
Luke 9:23	
Luke 12:29	
Luke 14:26	
Matt. 19:29	

DISCIPLES AND APOSTLES
QUALITIES OF DISCIPLESHIP (Cont.)

BIBLE VERSE	QUALITY
John 14:12	
John 8:31	
John 13:34-35	
John 15:8	
John 14:15, 21	

DISCIPLES AND APOSTLES
QUALITIES OF DISCIPLESHIP (Cont.)

BIBLE VERSE	QUALITY
Matt. 5:5, 44	
John 8:29	
Mark 14:36	
John 11:41	
Matt. 18:22	

DISCIPLES AND APOSTLES
QUALITIES OF DISCIPLESHIP (Cont.)

BIBLE VERSE	QUALITY
John 14:12	
Can you think of any more Bible verses which indicate qualities of a disciple? Add them to this list.	

DISCIPLES AND APOSTLES
ORIGIN OF THE GOSPELS

Before Mark set his pen to writing some 35 years after the events, memories of Jesus depended upon witnesses and those whom the witnesses told, in other words — "oral tradition."

This period of oral transmission contained stories about Jesus — certain events in his life and ministry and a collection of his sayings passed on by teachers to their listeners. The passion narrative — the Last Supper, Gethsemane, the arrest, trial, crucifixion, death and burial — was thought to be the first to take a definite form due to constant repetition. However, some scholars assert that quotes from the Old Testament which were thought to bear directly or indirectly on Jesus' life were first put into a series of testimonies.

While the apostles were alive, there was not much urgency to write down Jesus' sayings, since many expected his early return to earth. But, in Palestine in the middle of the first century, the pressures of Roman suppression were building to a crisis. Civil strife (especially among Jewish sects) was increasing, and border raids were a continual threat. As a result, many were leaving the country. At the same time, false teachings about Jesus were spreading rapidly. It is no wonder that the desire to preserve the pure, unadulterated sayings of the Master increased and careful attention to oral tradition became paramount. It is assumed that Jewish Christians, while fleeing Palestine, took with them fixed oral traditions, and soon found it necessary to put those traditions into writing for preservation.

How early did the sayings of Jesus begin to be written down? Probably not long after the Christian church moved into Greek-speaking countries. The Greeks loved to have things in writing. Professor C. H. Dodd calls these compilations of Jesus' sayings, "fly-sheets." The fly-sheets were brought together to form a comprehensive collection. Because there were many sayings in circulation, probably some were used in compiling the Gospels. These small blocks of material were most likely self-contained and were meant to convey some specific teaching with no chronology indicated. Nowhere in the Synoptic Gospels does the author reveal his identity.

(Sources: *About the Gospels*, C. H. Dodd; *The Interpreter's Dictionary of the Bible*; *Harper's Bible Dictionary*; *Anchor Bible* series, Vols. 26-29.)

DISCIPLES AND APOSTLES
THE FOUR GOSPELS

The Gospel According to
MARK

Many scholars believe this Gospel was the earliest of the four. It was written probably in Rome after the great fire of A.D. 64 by John Mark. His Gospel stands the closest in time to the actual events it is recording. John Mark was Paul's companion for awhile and the cousin of Barnabas. The first mention of John Mark is in Acts 12:12.

Eusebius (A.D. 270-340) quotes Papias (A.D. 60-130) in his book *Ecclesiastical History*, (Book III, 39.12-16): ". . . Mark became Peter's interpreter and wrote accurately all that he remembered, not, indeed, in order, of the things said or done by the Lord . . . so that Mark did nothing wrong in thus writing down single points as he remembered them. For to one thing he gave attention, to leave out nothing of what he had heard and to make no false statements in them."

It is possible that Mark translated Peter's Aramaic into Greek. Mark's Aramaic translations and explanations of Jewish customs suggest he was writing for a Greek audience. There is support for dating it after the death of Peter — Irenaeus substantiates this. Peter's death was during Nero's persecutions — A.D. 64-65. So the possible date for the Gospel is A.D. 64— some 35 years after the events it records.

I Peter 5:13 states Mark was with Peter in Rome. Mark's Gospel may have been written to sustain the faith of Christians living in Nero's Rome.

What lies behind Mark's Gospel is a living tradition — carefully guarded, constantly repeated. Knowledge depended on those who had witnessed the events and of those whom the witnesses told. C. H. Dodd explains that the early Christian community had a strong sense to publish its faith and felt a responsibility for telling the truth. They were like witnesses in court. Having grown up in a Jewish community where the teachings of the rabbis were preserved and transmitted by word of mouth, their memories were probably well-trained to be very accurate.

The secret to understanding the Gospels is the fact that the early Church centered its worship around remembering the facts about Jesus' life and living those facts. The first Christians believed with their whole heart that they had a story worth telling — what God had done for mankind.

DISCIPLES AND APOSTLES
THE FOUR GOSPELS (Cont.)

The Gospel According to
MATTHEW

Tradition says this Gospel was written by Matthew, the tax collector. Eusebius quotes Papias (*Ecclesiastical History*, Book III, 39.16), "Matthew collected the oracles in the Hebrew language, and each interpreted them as best he could." Eusebius also quotes Irenaeus: ". . . Matthew published among the Hebrews a written gospel also in their own tongue while Peter and Paul were preaching in Rome and founding the church" (op. cit., Book V, 8.2).

Some scholars say the basic source for Matthew was the Gospel according to Mark. He preserved almost the entire contents of Mark. (We might think of Matthew as a second edition of Mark, thoroughly revised.) Another source was the collection, oral or written, of Jesus' sayings which modern scholars call "Q" (German *Quelle* or source). It was an Aramaic collection that had already been translated into Greek and was possibly used by Luke and Matthew in its Greek form. This material contained many different traditions.

There seemed to be a need for a standard textbook or work of reference for teachers and pupils of his Jewish audience. The book needed authoritative backing — based on Jesus' teachings. Matthew was designed to supply this need. His material was based on collections from the private instruction of Jesus to the inner circle together with other material from his public teaching. Matthew grouped these teachings into five long discourses.

The Interpreter's Dictionary of the Bible (Vol. 3, p. 304) states, "The gospels do not rest upon the literary production of four men, or their own personal recollection, but upon the widespread social memory of the larger group, the whole Christian church, from its beginning, in the particular area where each gospel was finally produced."

There are over 60 Old Testament quotations in Matthew, not counting innumerable echoes of single words and phrases. Matthew continually refers to Old Testament authority for everything Jesus said and did.

Matthew was written in northern Palestine or Syria, maybe Antioch — where Judaism and Christianity still overlapped. When? Sometime after the fall of Jerusalem (A.D. 70), between A.D. 70-80.

DISCIPLES AND APOSTLES
THE FOUR GOSPELS (Cont.)

The Gospel According to
LUKE

Long-standing church tradition is that Luke, the physician and companion of Paul, is the author. Irenaeus wrote, "Luke, too, the companion of Paul, set forth in a book the gospel as preached by him." The Gospel is the first of a two-volume work on the beginnings of Christianity. The second volume is Acts of the Apostles.

Luke wrote his Gospel for Gentile converts — the educated Greek-speaking audiences of the empire. Most of Luke's Old Testament quotes are from the Greek version (the *Septuagint*). It has a missionary appeal. A probable date of its writing is between A.D. 70-80. It's anyone's guess as to where it was written. Scholars seem to be fairly certain it was not written in Palestine. Ancient tradition varies between Achaia, Boeotia, or Rome.

Luke's basic source material is Mark's Gospel — a major portion of Luke is the same as Mark. Then Luke maybe uses a collection of Jesus' sayings known as "Q." But there seems to be a third source — "L" — for material peculiar to Luke's Gospel and not found either in Mark or Matthew. But this source, scholars attest, is either oral or written and not on a scale with Mark or "Q."

Luke was dependent, too, on eyewitnesses. He was a great historian, researcher, and interviewer.

Luke 1:4 states the purpose of the book: "That thou mightest know the certainty of those things, wherein thou hast been instructed."

DISCIPLES AND APOSTLES
THE FOUR GOSPELS (Cont.)

The Gospel According to
JOHN

It was probably written in the Greek city of Ephesus by the beloved disciple, John (see John 21:20-24). Written not far from A.D. 100. "Irenaeus (ca. 180-200) says that after the writing of the other Gospels, John, the disciple of the Lord, ... published his Gospel at Ephesus" (*The Anchor Bible*, Vol. 29, LXXXVIII). Eusebius says Irenaeus received his information from Polycarp, who heard John.

It is possible that John read the other Gospels, but this is not known for certain. However, it is assumed that he was well-versed in the traditions and independent sources and saw something beneath merely the events tradition would relate.

John's aim is to give an interpretation of Jesus' life rather than another historical record. So Jesus is not merely a figure in ancient history, but a timeless representative.

According to C. H. Dodd, ". . . all the actions of Jesus that John records — and he gives only a small selection compared with the wealth of incidents in the other Gospels — are treated as 'signs,' or symbols, of some deeper truth" (*About the Gospels*, p. 39). John retold incidents in Jesus' life in such a way as to bring out the inner meaning of each of them. Clement of Alexandria called it the "spiritual gospel."

DISCIPLES AND APOSTLES
DISCIPLES — FISHERS OF MEN

SIMON PETER

Peter was a fisherman who could converse in Greek as well as Aramaic. He lived in Capernaum with his brother, Andrew. They were fishing partners with James and John. His original family home could be Bethsaida, but scholars aren't sure. The Synoptic Gospels place Peter's calling by Jesus near the Sea of Galilee, however, John places Peter's first contact with Jesus in Judaea near where John the Baptist was preaching. Andrew, who heard John the Baptist call Jesus "the Lamb of God," followed Jesus and came away convinced that Jesus was the Messiah. He told his brother, Peter, about it and brought him to Jesus (John 1:41).

At Caesarea Philippi, Peter recognized Jesus as the Christ, but failed to see in prophecy that the Messiah was to suffer. Some of Peter's travels included the Jerusalem Temple, Antioch (Syria), Asia Minor, Galatia, Rome, and maybe Corinth. Peter was married.

Some scholars believe he was the leader of the twelve disciples. He was also one of the inner circle with James and John which means he witnessed the raising of Jairus' daughter, the transfiguration, and was close to Jesus during the Gethsemane experience. He denied three times that he knew Jesus. He did not witness the crucifixion. His original name was Simon, but Jesus gave him the name Peter (the Greek word is *petros* — or "rock"). Cephas is Aramaic for "rock." Tradition says he was crucified upside down in Nero's Rome in A.D. 64 or 67. Mark's Gospel is possibly the reminiscences of Peter. The book of I Peter is also attributed to Peter.

DISCIPLES AND APOSTLES
DISCIPLES — FISHERS OF MEN (Cont.)

ANDREW (Greek name)

Andrew was the brother of Simon Peter and their original home was thought to be Bethsaida. He probably followed John the Baptist before becoming one of Jesus' disciples. According to John's Gospel, he was the first to recognize Jesus as the Messiah. He brought his brother, Simon Peter, to meet Jesus. Andrew's nature was thought to be pliable and teachable, humble, and generous. Andrew was a fisherman who lived in Capernaum.

He was the disciple who called to Jesus' attention the lad with five barley loaves and two fish when Jesus was addressing the multitude. Later in Jesus' ministry he brought Greeks to Jesus (John 12:20-22). Andrew's travels included Scythia (the region north of the Black Sea). Tradition says he suffered martyrdom by crucifixion in Greece.

JAMES (Brother of John)

James' family home may also have been Bethsaida. He was a fisherman on the Sea of Galilee and a partner with John, Peter, and Andrew. Like John, James was named one of the "sons of thunder" by Jesus. James was included in the inner circle of disciples who witnessed the raising of Jairus' daughter, the transfiguration, and Jesus' Gethsemane experience. James' martyrdom is the only one mentioned in the New Testament. He probably was the first to be put to death (Acts 12:1-3) in A.D. 44 by Herod Agrippa I.

JAMES (Son of Alphaeus)

This disciple is not mentioned by name in any event recorded in the Gospels or Acts of the Apostles. It is possible that this James is to be identified as one of the sons of Mary, who is mentioned as present at the crucifixion and the empty tomb.

DISCIPLES AND APOSTLES
DISCIPLES — FISHERS OF MEN (Cont.)

JOHN (Brother of James)

John was a fisherman on the Sea of Galilee with his brother and a partner with Peter and Andrew. He was from a well-to-do family who had "hired servants." The family home originally may have been in Bethsaida. His mother, Salome, was a follower of Jesus. According to Matthew's version, she tried to rearrange the seating in heaven for her sons to be on the right and left side of Jesus. Salome also witnessed the crucifixion. John lived near Capernaum; but after A.D. 70, he probably lived in Ephesus, according to Irenaeus. While mending their nets, the brothers were called by Jesus in Galilee. They were part of the inner circle of disciples closest to Jesus which means they witnessed the raising of Jairus' daughter, the transfiguration, and the Gethsemane experience before Jesus' arrest. Jesus gave the two brothers the name "sons of thunder." Tradition says John wrote the Gospel of John, I, II, and III John, and the book of Revelation (written on the isle of Patmos around A.D. 95). He's the disciple pictured at the Last Supper as leaning on Jesus' breast. John is the only disciple to witness the crucifixion. Jesus entrusted his mother to John. John ran with Peter to witness an empty tomb. Tertullian (A.D. 145-200) says John was boiled in oil, then banished to Patmos. John, in his old age, repeatedly told Christians in their meetings, "Little children, love one another" (Jerome, *Commentary on Galatians*). Eusebius quotes Apollonius that John raised the dead at Ephesus.

MATTHEW

Matthew was a tax collector in the service of Herod Antipas near Capernaum before he became a disciple. He worked in a profession that was much hated among the Jews. His Gospel mentions that he left the receipt of custom and followed Jesus (Matt. 9:9). Luke mentions that Levi entertained Jesus and other tax collectors in his home (Luke 5:29). Early church tradition assigns Matthew as the author of the Gospel of Matthew written for Jews.

DISCIPLES AND APOSTLES
DISCIPLES — FISHERS OF MEN (Cont.)

THOMAS (In Aramaic means "twin"; [Didymus in Greek])

Thomas is mentioned three times in the Gospel of John: John 11:16 indicates his loyalty to Jesus; John 14:5 shows his ignorance of Jesus' meaning about preparing a place for them; John 20:24-28 reveals his doubting nature when he has to touch the wounds after the resurrection before he will believe. Eusebius mentions Thomas as traveling to Parthia (Persia). The Acts of Thomas (written in the 3rd or 4th century) mention that he was martyred in India. A Gospel of Thomas found in the sands of Egypt contains collections or sayings attributed to Jesus. Possibly much of the material was written within ten or 20 years of Jesus' ascension. Its Greek text may have been produced about A.D. 140.

JUDAS ISCARIOT

Judas Iscariot is the only Judaean of the twelve disciples. "Iscariot" could mean "man from Kerioth" (though it is uncertain as to where this is located). He was the treasurer of the group (John 13:29). He betrayed Jesus to the chief priests for 30 pieces of silver. No one knows exactly why. Many speculations surround the event. A plot of ground, a "potter's field," was purchased with the money. It is even questionable whether Judas participated in the taking of bread and wine at the Last Supper. Luke says he did; other Gospels leave us in doubt. He died a violent death; Matthew tells us he hanged himself.

JUDAS (Thaddaeus)

Luke has this disciple as the son or brother of James (Luke 6:16). Thaddaeus may be his true name.

DISCIPLES AND APOSTLES
DISCIPLES — FISHERS OF MEN (Cont.)

PHILIP (Greek name)

In the Gospel of John, Philip was one of the first to be called. His hometown was possibly Bethsaida. Philip tells Nathanael, ". . . We have found him, of whom Moses in the law, and the prophets, did write, Jesus of Nazareth, . . ." (John 1:45). His name is mentioned in connection with the feeding of the five thousand. Philip asks Jesus, ". . . Lord, shew us the Father, and it sufficeth us" (John 14:8). Philip was asked by the Greek-speaking Jews to help them see Jesus.

NATHANAEL (Bartholomew)

This disciple was from Cana in Galilee. He was brought by Philip to Jesus. He showed skepticism when Philip described Jesus as the Messiah and from Nazareth. Nathanael asked, "Can there any good thing come out of Nazareth?" (John 1:46) Jesus described Nathanael as an Israelite in whom there is no guile. He is mentioned in the Gospel of John as Nathanael, but as Bartholomew (son of Talmai) in the Synoptics. He promptly declared his faith that Jesus is the Son of God after meeting the Master (John 1:49).

SIMON THE ZEALOT

Simon was formerly of the fanatical Zealots who opposed Roman rule in Palestine. He is mentioned only when the disciples are listed in the Gospels. Early Christian writers say he is the same Simeon, son of Clopas, who succeeded James as head of the Jerusalem church (Eusebius, *Ecclesiastical History*, Book III, 11.32).

DISCIPLES AND APOSTLES
APOSTLES

JOHN MARK

John Mark was the son of Mary of Jerusalem (Acts 12:12), a companion of Paul on his first journey, and cousin of Barnabas. Many scholars believe he is the author of the Gospel of Mark. Tradition says that the Last Supper was held at the house of his mother, but the Gospels do not support this. John Mark might have been a witness to some of the final events in Jesus' life; however, Papias records that Mark "had neither heard the Lord nor been his personal follower" (Eusebius, *Ecclesiastical History*, Book III, 39.15). John Mark was probably a close associate of Peter's in Rome. Eusebius quotes Papias as saying that Mark was Peter's "interpreter" and that he wrote down what Peter had said (ibid.). Tradition says Mark was the founder of Alexandrian Christianity; it also states he suffered a martyr's death. The Gospel was probably written in Rome for a Gentile audience.

LUKE

According to tradition, Luke was a Syrian of Antioch, who wrote a Gospel derived from Paul. He wrote it either in Achaia, Rome, or Bithynia. Tradition says he died in Boeotia or Thebes at the age of 84. Luke was a physician and companion of Paul, but did not witness Jesus' ministry firsthand. His Gospel was written for Gentile converts. He is also thought to be the author of the book of Acts. The Gospel of Luke indicates that the author was a researcher who interviewed eyewitnesses to the events of Jesus' life.

STEPHEN

Stephen, in the book of Acts, is described as ". . . a man full of faith and of the Holy Ghost . . ." (Acts 6:5); and one who ". . . did great wonders and miracles among the people" (Acts 6:8). He was selected by the disciples to remedy the neglect of the widows by supervising this charity work. He was stoned at the hand of the Jews — making him the first Christian martyr.

DISCIPLES AND APOSTLES
APOSTLES (Cont.)

JAMES (Brother of Jesus)

James, the brother of Jesus, was apparently not a disciple during Jesus' ministry; although according to I Corinthians he did witness the resurrection. He became head of the church in Jerusalem. It is possible that he is the author of the Letter of James, though no one is certain. It appears that he was devoted to Jewish tradition. According to Eusebius, James spent so much time on his knees in intercession for the people that his knees grew callous like a camel's (*Ecclesiastical History*, Book II, 23.4-18). According to Josephus, James was put to death in the early sixties at the order of the high priest.

PAUL

Paul was born in Tarsus in Cilicia with the name of Saul. His trade was tenting, but he became a student of the law under the teaching of Gamaliel. According to Acts, he was a Pharisee who persecuted the Jerusalem church. He witnessed the stoning of Stephen. His conversion occurred on the road to Damascus after Jesus' ascension. He then called himself "an apostle to the Gentiles." He founded churches in Greece and Asia Minor and wrote many letters to these new churches as he traveled.

BIBLE TIME LINE

CONTENTS:

- Time Line
- Events Lists
- Dates of Roman Emperors
- Background of Dates

MATERIALS:

- Time Line
- Scissors/Tape

MEMORY VERSE:

". . . Ye do err, not knowing the scriptures, nor the power of God."

Matthew 22:29

Bible Time Line
BACKGROUND DATES IN BIBLICAL HISTORY

You will discover in your own research that scholars do not always agree on Biblical dates. However, it is important for students to understand historical events in relation to one another in order to gain a broad overview of important happenings in the Biblical world before, during, and after Jesus' arrival on the human scene.

As an example, there was an error in the calculation of the Christian era due to Dionysius Exiguus in the sixth century. He miscalculated the birth of Jesus by several years.

The dates on the following pages have been generally accepted by many scholars. However in some cases, there are significant differences of opinion. No one knows for sure an exact date for many of the events. The sources used for compiling this list are *Dictionary of Proper Names and Places in the Bible* by O. Odelain and R. Séguneau, *Light From the Ancient Past* by Jack Finegan, and several Bible dictionaries.

Directions: Tape the Time Line sheets together to make one long sheet. (If you are working with young children, use only 10-15 important dates.) Then cut out events and dates from the Events List and glue or tape them onto the Time Line. Hang the Time Line up so it can be used as a reference for further study.

It is also recommended that the Time Line be color-coded. The students can either highlight the strips in colors or write out their own time line with color markers.

Sample color scheme:
- Herod dates — Green
- Roman dates — Red
- Jesus' dates — Blue
- Christianity dates — Purple
- Books written in the New Testament — Brown

Bible Time Line
CHRONOLOGICAL DATES

63 B.C. _____

55 B.C. _____

51-30 B.C. _____

37 B.C. _____

27 B.C. _____

20/19 B.C. _____

8-6 B.C. _____

4 B.C. _____

A.D. 5-10 (A.D. 1) _____

A.D. 6 _____

A.D. 14-37 _____

A.D. 26-36 _____

A.D. 26-27 _____

A.D. 27-28 _____

A.D. 29-30 _____

A.D. 36-37 _____

A.D. 37 _____

A.D. 37-38 _____

A.D. 39 _____

A.D. 45-49 _____

A.D. 50-52 _____

Bible Time Line
CHRONOLOGICAL DATES (Cont.)

A.D. 53-58 _____

A.D. 54-57 _____

A.D. 56 _____

A.D. 57 _____

A.D. 57-58 _____

A.D. 58 (some say 125-150) _____

A.D. 61-63 _____

A.D. 62 _____

A.D. 64 _____

A.D. 64 or 67 _____

A.D. 65 _____

A.D. 66 _____

A.D. 67 _____

A.D. 70 _____

A.D. 70-80 _____

A.D. 73 _____

A.D. 93 _____

A.D. 93-96 _____

A.D. 95-96 _____

A.D. 95-115 _____

A.D. 98-115 _____

Bible Time Line

CHRONOLOGICAL DATES (Cont.)

A.D. 270 _____

A.D. 313 _____

A.D. 324 _____

A.D. 325 _____

A.D. 339 or 340 _____

Bible Time Line
EVENTS LIST

Pompey, Roman general, invades Palestine
and establishes Roman rule (63 B.C.)

Herod Antipater (father of Herod the Great)
becomes ruler in Palestine by Roman grant (55 B.C.)

Cleopatra VII, Queen of Egypt (51-30 B.C.)

Herod the Great, King of Judaea under the Romans (37 B.C.)

Roman Emperor Caesar Augustus begins his reign (27 B.C.)

Herod the Great begins rebuilding the Jewish Temple (20/19 B.C.)

Birth of Jesus (8-6 B.C.)

Herod the Great dies (4 B.C.)

Birth of Paul (between A.D. 5-10; some say A.D. 1)

Roman Emperor Tiberius reigns (A.D. 14-37)

Pontius Pilate, Roman procurator, rules Palestine
for the Romans (A.D. 26-36)

Beginning of Jesus' ministry (A.D. 26-27)

Baptism of Jesus (A.D. 27-28)

Crucifixion of Jesus; Pentecost (A.D. 29-30)

Stoning of Stephen (A.D. 36-37)

Conversion of Paul (A.D. 36-37)

Bible Time Line
EVENTS LIST (Cont.)

Death of Tiberius (A.D. 37)

Birth of Josephus (A.D. 37 or 38)

Herod Antipas deposed (A.D. 39)

Paul's first missionary journey (A.D. 45-49)

Paul's second missionary journey (A.D. 50-52)

Thessalonian letters (A.D. 50-52)

Paul's third missionary journey (A.D. 53-58)

Letter to the Galatians (A.D. 54-57)

Letter to the Philippians (A.D. 56?)

Letter to the Corinthians (A.D. 57)

Letter to the Romans (A.D. 57-58)

Letter of James (A.D. 58; some say 125-150)

Ephesians; Colossians; Philemon (A.D. 61-63)

Martyrdom of James (A.D. 62)

Gospel of Mark; I Peter (A.D. 64)

Peter's martyrdom (A.D. 64 or 67)

I Timothy; Titus (A.D. 65)

Jewish Revolt (A.D. 66)

Bible Time Line
EVENTS LIST (Cont.)

II Timothy; Letter to the Hebrews (A.D. 67)

Paul beheaded (A.D. 67)

Titus lays siege to Jerusalem (A.D. 70)

Gospel of Matthew; Gospel of Luke; Acts; Jude; II Peter (A.D. 70-80). (Some scholars have an earlier date for Acts — early A.D. 60s, and some scholars have a much later date for II Peter — A.D. 98 or 150.)

Fall of Masada (A.D. 73)

Antiquities of the Jews, by Josephus (A.D. 93)

Persecutions of the Christians under Emperor Domitian (A.D. 93-96)

Book of Revelation (A.D. 95-96)

Gospel of John (A.D. 95-115)

Johannine Epistles (A.D. 98-115)

Birth of Eusebius (A.D. 270)

Constantine proclaims Christianity the religion of the Roman world (A.D. 313)

End of Roman rule in Palestine (A.D. 324)

Council of Nicea (A.D. 325)

Death of Eusebius (A.D. 339 or 340)

Bible Time Line

DATES OF THE ROMAN EMPERORS

Julius Caesar, dictator . . . . 49-44 B.C.
Caesar Augustus 27-B.C.-A.D. 14
Tiberius . . . . A.D. 14-37
Claudius 41-54
Nero 54-68
Galba 68-69
Otho . . . . 69 (3 months)
Vitellius . . . . 69 (1 month)
Vespasian 69-79
Titus 79-81
Domitian 81-96
Nerva 96-98
Trajan 98-117
Hadrian 117-138
Antonius Pius 138-161
Marcus Aurelius 161-180
Commodus 180-192
Septimus Severus 193-211
Alexander Severus 222-235

In the years from Alexander Severus to Aurelian,
37 men were proclaimed emperors.

Aurelian 270-275
Tacitus . . . . 275 (6 months)
Probus 276-282
Diocletian 282-305
Constantine I The Great (Emperor of the West) . 305-337
Galerius (Emperor of the East) 305-311
Julian the Apostate 361-363
Romulus Augustulus (last Emperor of the West) . 475-476
Justinian I 527-565
Constantine XI (last Emperor of the East) 1449-1453

BIBLE TERMS AND GREEK VOCABULARY

CONTENTS:

- Bible Terms
- Greek Vocabulary
- Flash Cards

MATERIALS:

- Bible
- Bible Dictionary
- Strong's Bible Concordance
- Activity Sheets

MEMORY VERSE:

"Judge not according to the appearance, but judge righteous judgment."

John 7:24

Bible Terms and Greek Vocabulary
BIBLE TERMS

Directions: Look in a Bible dictionary and write the definition of each word in the blank. Make flash cards to study the words and definitions. Some words may be found in the Glossary at the back of this book.

1. synagogue _____

_____

2. scribe _____

_____

3. parable _____

_____

4. tares _____

_____

5. Galilee _____

_____

6. Magi _____

_____

7. Passover _____

_____

8. publican _____

_____

9. moneychanger _____

_____

Bible Terms and Greek Vocabulary
BIBLE TERMS (Cont.)

10. Temple _____

_____

11. Gentile _____

_____

12. Jew _____

_____

13. papyrus _____

_____

14. scroll _____

_____

15. prophet _____

_____

16. rabbi _____

_____

17. Aramaic _____

_____

18. Greek _____

_____

19. Samaritan _____

_____

_____

Bible Terms and Greek Vocabulary
BIBLE TERMS (Cont.)

20. Hebrew _____

_____

21. crucifixion _____

_____

22. Messiah _____

_____

23. talent _____

_____

24. Saviour _____

_____

25. Beelzebub _____

_____

26. Levi _____

_____

_____

_____

_____

_____

_____

Bible Terms and Greek Vocabulary
GREEK VOCABULARY

Directions: In the list below, look up each word in Strong's *Exhaustive Bible Concordance*; then find the Bible verse (in parentheses) where the word is used. In the right-hand column of Strong's Concordance, see what corresponding number is used in Strong's *Greek Dictionary*. Turn to the *Greek Dictionary* found in the back of Strong's and find the number. (Remember the exercise in Lesson Packet 1 which showed students how to read the number and then look it up.) Write down the original Greek meaning behind the word used by the translators. Then read the verse again in the context of the original Greek meaning.

Another good reference book is *Thayer's Greek-English Lexicon*. Its numbers correspond with Strong's. The answers are also found in the Teacher's Notes at the end of this Lesson Packet on pages 91-94.

1. again (John 3:3) _____

_____

2. lovest (John 21:15)

_____

3. love (John 21:15) _____

_____

4. Comforter (John 14:16) _____

_____

5. rock (Matt. 16:18) _____

_____

6. Word (John 1:1) _____

_____

Bible Terms and Greek Vocabulary
GREEK VOCABULARY (Cont.)

7. disciples (John 8:31)_____

_____

8. Christ (Matt. 16:16)_____

_____

9. apostles (Matt. 10:2)_____

_____

10. gospel (Mark 1:1) _____

_____

11. Ghost (Luke 3:22) _____

_____

12. miracle (John 4:54) _____

_____

13. sin (John 1:29) _____

_____

14. sleep (Luke 9:32) _____

_____

15. Lord (Mark 10:51) _____

_____

16. Watch (Mark 13:37) _____

_____

Bible Terms and Greek Vocabulary
GREEK VOCABULARY (Cont.)

17. Amen (Matt. 28:20) _____

_____

18. Satan (Matt. 4:10) _____

_____

19. Blessed (Matt. 5:5) _____

_____

20. hypocrite (Luke 13:15) _____

_____

21. Repent (Matt. 3:2) _____

**For further study, look up the original
Greek meaning of the following words.**

1. fornication _____

_____

2. witchcraft _____

_____

3. sorcerers _____

_____

4. sorceries _____

_____

ACTIVITY SHEET

Bible Terms and Greek Vocabulary
GREEK VOCABULARY (Cont.)

5. judgment _____

_____

6. baptize _____

_____

7. Gethsemane _____

_____

8. closet _____

_____

9. beginning _____

_____

10. save or salvation _____

_____

11. glory _____

_____

synagogue	scribe	parable
tares	Galilee	Magi
Passover	publican	moneychanger
Temple	Gentile	Jew
papyrus	scroll	prophet
Rabbi	Aramaic	Greek
Samaritan	Hebrew	crucifixion

Messiah	talent	Saviour
Beelzebub	Levi	anothen
agapao	phileo	Parakletos
petra	logos	mathetes
Christos	apostolos	pneuma
semeion	hupnos	makarios
hupokrites	metanoeo	Amen

Bible Terms and Greek Vocabulary
GREEK VOCABULARY

1. John 3:3: ". . . ye must born **again.**"

   Greek word is **anothen** (an'-o-then) — "from above, from a higher place." Used for things which come from heaven or from God as dwelling in heaven.

2. John 21:15: ". . . Jesus saith unto Simon Peter, Simon, son of Jonas, **lovest** thou me more than these?"

   Greek word is **agapao** (ag-ap-ah'-o) — spiritual sense of love; affectionate reverence; be unwilling to abandon it; to desire good for someone you esteem.

3. John 21:15: Peter answers Jesus, ". . . Yea, Lord; thou knowest that I **love** thee."

   Greek word is **phileo** (fil-eh'-o) — to be a friend; denoting personal attachment.

4. John 14:16: "And I will pray the Father, and he shall give you another **Comforter,** that he may abide with you for ever;"

   Greek word is **parakletos** (par-ak'-lay-tos) — called to one's aid; an advocate; defense attorney (one who pleads another's cause before a judge).

5. Matt. 16:18: ". . . thou art Peter, and upon this **rock** I will build my church; . . ."

   Greek word is **petra** - feminine (pet'-ra) — a stone; rock.

6. John 1:1: "In the beginning was the **Word,** and the **Word** was with God, and the **Word** was God."

   Greek word is **logos** (log'-os) — word which embodies a conception or idea; the mental faculty of thinking; reasoning; those things gathered together in mind and expressed as words.

Bible Terms and Greek Vocabulary
GREEK VOCABULARY (Cont.)

7. John 8:31: "Then said Jesus . . . If ye continue in my word, then ye are my *disciples* indeed;"

   Greek word is *mathetes* (math-ay-tes') — a learner; a pupil; one who practices what he learns.

8. Matt. 16:16: ". . . Thou art the *Christ*, the Son of the living God."

   Greek word is *Christos* (khris-tos') — anointed one.

9. Matt. 10:2: "Now the names of the twelve *apostle*s are these; . . ."

   Greek word is *apostolos* (ap-os'-tol-os) — one who is sent forth with orders, messenger, specifically an ambassador of the Gospel.

10. Mark 1:1: "The beginning of the *gospel* of Jesus Christ, . . ."

    A combination of two Greek words — *eu* meaning "from" and *angelos* meaning "messengers" — good news of victory (C. H. Dodd); glad tidings; good message.

11. Luke 3:22: "And the Holy *Ghost* descended in a bodily shape like a dove upon him, . . ."

    Greek word is *pneuma* (pnyoo'-mah) — breath; movement of air; wind; spirit; ghost; to breathe out the spirit.

12. John 4:54: "This is again the second *miracle* that Jesus did, . . ."

    Greek word is *semeion* (say-mi'-on) — sign; mark; wonders by which men prove that the cause they are pleading is God's.

Bible Terms and Greek Vocabulary
GREEK VOCABULARY (Cont.)

13. John 1:29: ". . . Behold the Lamb of God, which taketh away the *sin* of the world."

    Greek word is *hamartia* (ham-ar-tee'-ah) — a failing to hit the mark; an error of understanding.

14. Luke 9:32: "But Peter and they that were with him were heavy with *sleep* . . ."

    Greek word is *hupnos* (hoop'-nos) — sleep; spiritual torpor; the word "hypnotic" is derived from this Greek word.

15. Mark 10:51: ". . . The blind man said unto him, *Lord*, that I might receive my sight."

    Greek word is *rhabboni* — highest title of honor in Jewish schools; master; chief. Only used one other time in the Gospels — John 20:16 — when Mary addresses Jesus after the resurrection.

16. Mark 13:37: "And what I say unto you I say unto all, *Watch*.

    Greek word is *gregoreuo* (gray-gor-yoo'-o) — to watch; to give strict attention to; be cautious; active; to be awake; to have been roused from sleep.

17. Matt. 28:20: ". . . I am with you alway, even unto the end of the world. *Amen*."

    Greek word is *amen* (am-ane') — so be it; of a truth; something confirmed; may it be fulfilled.

Bible Terms and Greek Vocabulary
GREEK VOCABULARY (Cont.)

18. Matt. 4:10: "Then saith Jesus unto him, Get thee hence, *Satan*: . . ."

    Greek word is *satanas* (sat-an-as') or *satan* — accuser; adversary; one who opposes another in purpose or act.

19. Matt. 5:5: "*Blessed* are the meek: for they shall inherit the earth."

    Greek word is *makarios* (mak-ar'-ee-os) — happy from within.

20. Luke 13:15: ". . . Thou *hypocrite*, doth not each one of you on the sabbath loose his ox or his ass from the stall, and lead him away to watering?"

    Greek word is *hupokrites* (hoop-ok-ree-tace') — actor under an assumed character; pretender.

21. Matt. 3:2: ". . . *Repent* ye: for the kingdom of heaven is at hand."

    Greek word is *metanoeo* (mat-an-o-eh-o) — to change one's mind for the better; to think differently.

JESUS' THREE-YEAR MINISTRY

CONTENTS:

- Terrritory Divisions Map
- Gospel Record of Jesus' Ministry

MATERIALS:

- Bible
- Bible Concordance
- Activity Sheets

MEMORY VERSE:

". . . seek ye first the kingdom of God, and his righteousness; and all these things shall be added unto you."

Matthew 6:33

EVENTS IN JESUS' MINISTRY

Directions: Use the Teacher's Notes to fill in the Activity Sheets together. Talk about how the events are approximate. The "periods" are terms some Bible scholars use to distinguish Jesus' ministry. Remember that some scholars feel there was only a one-year ministry; others think there were only two.

For older students:
Use a Bible concordance to find New Testament verses to verify the event.

Jesus' Three-Year Ministry
EVENTS IN JESUS' MINISTRY

A.D. 26-27 — What opened Jesus' Ministry?   Verses to verify events

_____   _____

_____   _____

_____   _____

_____   _____

_____   _____

_____   _____

What happened in the early   Verses to verify events
Judaean Ministry of Jesus?

_____   _____

_____   _____

_____   _____

_____   _____

_____   _____

Jesus' Three-Year Ministry
EVENTS IN JESUS' MINISTRY (Cont.)

FIRST PERIOD

Galilean Ministry —
What were Jesus' healings?

Verses to verify events

_____   _____

_____   _____

_____   _____

_____   _____

_____   _____

_____   _____

_____   _____

FIRST PERIOD

Galilean Ministry —
What other events took place?

Verses to verify events

_____   _____

_____   _____

_____   _____

_____   _____

_____   _____

_____   _____

Jesus' Three-Year Ministry
EVENTS IN JESUS' MINISTRY (Cont.)

FIRST PERIOD

Galilean Ministry —
What parables did Jesus give?   Verses to verify events

_____   _____

_____   _____

SECOND PERIOD

Galilean Ministry —
What healings occurred?   Verses to verify events

_____   _____

_____   _____

_____   _____

_____   _____

_____   _____

_____   _____

_____   _____

_____   _____

_____   _____

_____   _____

Jesus' Three-Year Ministry
EVENTS IN JESUS' MINISTRY (Cont.)

SECOND PERIOD

Galilean Ministry —   Verses to verify events
What other incidents took place?

_____   _____

_____   _____

_____   _____

_____   _____

_____   _____

_____   _____

_____   _____

_____   _____

Jesus' Three-Year Ministry
EVENTS IN JESUS' MINISTRY (Cont.)

SECOND PERIOD

Galilean Ministry —
What parables were given?

Verses to verify events

_____   _____

_____   _____

_____   _____

_____   _____

_____   _____

_____   _____

_____   _____

_____   _____

Jesus' Three-Year Ministry
EVENTS IN JESUS' MINISTRY (Cont.)

THIRD PERIOD

Galilean Ministry —
What healings came about?

Verses to verify events

_____   _____

_____   _____

_____   _____

_____   _____

_____   _____

_____   _____

_____   _____

THIRD PERIOD

Galilean Ministry —
Name the parable given by Jesus.

Verse to verify events

_____   _____

Jesus' Three-Year Ministry
EVENTS IN JESUS' MINISTRY (Cont.)

PERAEAN PERIOD

Last few months —
What healings were accomplished?

Verses to verify events

_____   _____

_____   _____

_____   _____

_____   _____

_____   _____

_____   _____

PERAEAN PERIOD

What other events took place?

Verses to verify events

_____   _____

_____   _____

_____   _____

Jesus' Three-Year Ministry
TERRITORY DIVISIONS MAP

Directions: Use the filled-in Territory Divisions Map. Find at least one event that happened in each territory and write it out below with a corresponding Bible verse. You will need to use a Bible concordance.

Territories

Decapolis	Peraea
Judaea	Galilee
Samaria	Idumaea
Phoenicia	

Decapolis _____

Judaea _____

Samaria _____

Phoenicia _____

Peraea _____

Galilee _____

Idumaea _____

Jesus' Three-Year Ministry
TERRITORY DIVISIONS MAP
(Filled-In)

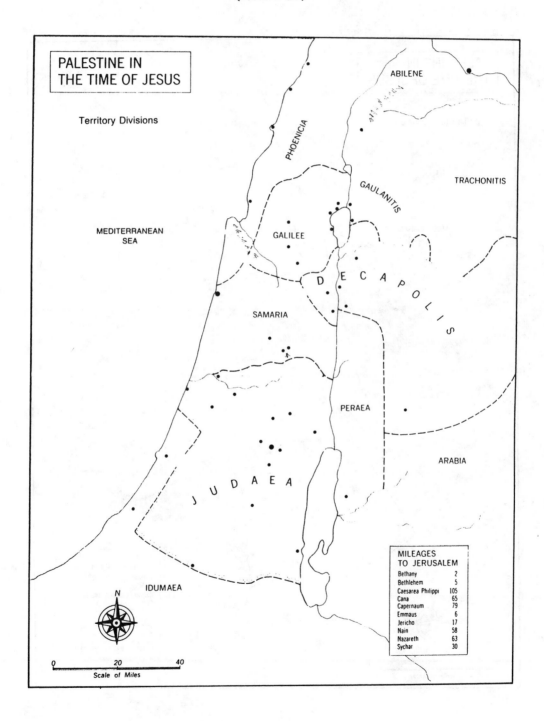

PALESTINE IN
THE TIME OF JESUS

Territory Divisions

ABILENE

PHOENICIA

TRACHONITIS

GAULANITIS

GALILEE

MEDITERRANEAN
SEA

D E C A P O L I S

SAMARIA

PERAEA

ARABIA

J U D A E A

N

IDUMAEA

MILEAGES TO JERUSALEM	
Bethany	2
Bethlehem	5
Caesarea Philippi	105
Cana	65
Capernaum	79
Emmaus	6
Jericho	17
Nain	58
Nazareth	63
Sychar	30

0   20   40
Scale of Miles

Jesus' Three-Year Ministry
TERRITORY DIVISIONS MAP
(Blank)

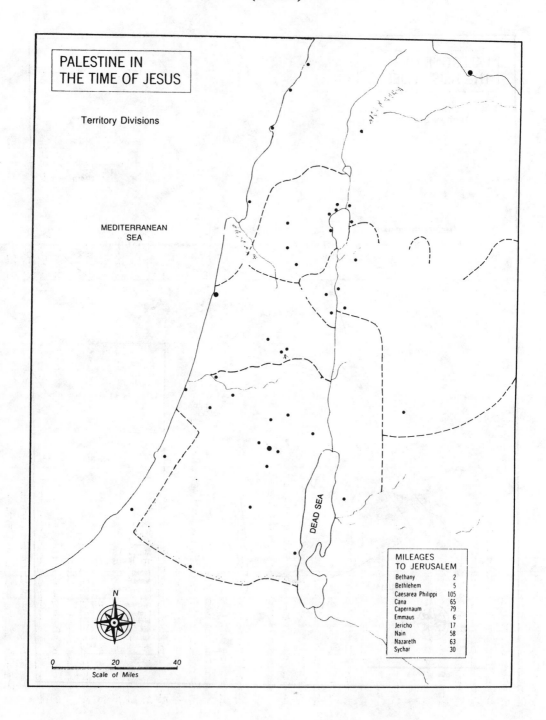

PALESTINE IN
THE TIME OF JESUS

Territory Divisions

MEDITERRANEAN
SEA

DEAD SEA

MILEAGES TO JERUSALEM	
Bethany	2
Bethlehem	5
Caesarea Philippi	105
Cana	65
Capernaum	79
Emmaus	6
Jericho	17
Nain	58
Nazareth	63
Sychar	30

N

0   20   40
Scale of Miles

JESUS' THREE-YEAR MINISTRY
THE GOSPEL RECORD OF JESUS' MINISTRY

	Matthew	Mark	Luke	John
Opening Events of Jesus' Ministry				
Ministry of John the Baptist	3:1-12	1:1-13	3:1-18	—
Baptism of Jesus	3:13-17	1:9-11	3:21-23	—
Jesus' Temptation in wilderness	4:1-11	1:12-13	4:1-13	—
John the Baptist's testimony of Christ	—	—	—	1:19-28
Jesus called "Lamb of God"	—	—	—	1:29-34
The first disciples — Andrew, Peter, Philip, Nathanael	—	—	—	1:35-51
The first miracle — water made wine	—	—	—	2:1-11
Early Judaean Ministry of Jesus				
Passover time in Jerusalem:				
First cleansing of the Temple	—	—	—	2:13-22
First discourse: the new birth	—	—	—	3:1-21
Jesus' disciples baptize in Judaea	—	—	—	3:22; 4:1-2
John the Baptist's doctrine concerning Christ	—	—	—	3:23-36
John the Baptist imprisoned by Herod	4:12	1:14	3:19-20	—
In Samaria: Jesus meets woman at the well; Jesus confesses to her he is the Messiah	—	—	—	4:1-42
First Period — Galilean Ministry				
Preaching and fame	4:12-17	1:14-15	4:14-15	4:43-45
Healing of the nobleman's son	—	—	—	4:46-54
First rejection at Nazareth, escape from brow of hill	—	—	4:16-30	—
Jesus dwells in Capernaum	4:13-16	—	4:31	—
Call of the Four, great draft of fishes	4:18-22	1:16-20	5:1-11	—
Healing of man with unclean spirit	—	1:21-28	4:31-37	—
Healing of Peter's wife's mother	8:14-17	1:29-34	4:38-41	—
Preaching and healing in Galilee	4:23-25	1:35-39	4:42-44	—
Healing of a leper	8:1-4	1:40-45	5:12-16	—
Healing of a paralytic	9:1-8	2:1-12	5:17-26	—
Accusation of blasphemy				
The call of Matthew (Levi)	9:9-13	2:13-17	5:27-32	—
Question about observance of fasting	9:14-17	2:18-22	5:33-39	—
Parable of new cloth on old garment	9:16	2:21	5:36	—
Parable of new wine in old bottles	9:17	2:22	5:37-39	—

THE PASSION NARRATIVE
THE GOSPEL RECORD OF JESUS' MINISTRY (Cont.)

	Matthew	Mark	Luke	John
In Jerusalem:				
Healing of man at pool of Bethesda	—	—	—	5:1-15
Jesus accused of blasphemy	—	—	—	5:16-18
Discourse: the Son and the Father	—	—	—	5:19-47
In Galilee:				
Disciples pluck grain on sabbath	12:1-8	2:23-28	6:1-5	—
Healing of a man with a withered hand	12:9-14	3:1-6	6:6-11	—
Widening popularity due to his healing activity	12:15-21	3:7-12	—	—
Second Period — Galilean Ministry				
Ordaining 12 apostles to preach and heal	—	3:13-19	6:12-19	—
Discourse: the Sermon on the Mount	5-7	—	6:20-49	—
Parable of house built on rock, on sand	7:24-27	—	6:47-49	—
Healing centurion's servant	8:5-13	—	7:1-10	—
Raising of the widow's son at Nain	—	—	7:11-17	—
Answer to John the Baptist's questions	11:2-30	—	7:18-35	—
Discourse: Woes on impenitent cities, Christ's invitation to the weary	11:20-30	—	—	—
Healing of a penitent sinner	—	—	7:36-50	—
Parable of two debtors	—	—	7:41-50	—
Women minister to Jesus	—	—	8:1-3	—
Healing of a man blind and dumb	12:22-45	3:20-30	11:14 (?)	—
Accusation of the Pharisees: blasphemy against the Holy Ghost				
Jesus declares his true family	12:46-50	3:31-35	8:19-21	—
Parables of the kingdom of heaven: sower, seed, tares, mustard seed, leaven, hidden treasure, pearl, dragnet	13:1-53	4:1-34	8:4-18; 13:18-21	—
Stilling the tempest	8:18, 23-27	4:35-41	8:22-25	—
Healing of the Gadarene demoniac	8:28-34	5:1-20	8:26-39	—
Raising of Jairus' daughter	9:18-26	5:21-43	8:40-56	—
Healing of a woman with issue of blood	9:20-22	5:25-34	8:43-48	—
Healing of two blind men	9:27-31	—	—	—
Healing of dumb demoniac	9:32-34	—	—	—

JESUS' THREE-YEAR MINISTRY
THE GOSPEL RECORD OF JESUS' MINISTRY (Cont.)

	Matthew	Mark	Luke	John
Second rejection at Nazareth	13:54-58	6:1-6	—	—
Commissioning of the Twelve	9:35-11:1	6:7-13	9:1-6	—
The martyrdom of John the Baptist	14:1-12	6:14-29	9:7-9	—
Feeding of the five thousand	14:13-23	6:30-46	9:10-17	6:1-14
People want to make Jesus a king	—	—	—	6:15
Walks on the sea; his ship immediately at the other side of the lake	14:24-36	6:47-56	—	6:16-21
Discourse: Christ the bread of life	—	—	—	6:22-71
Discourse: against traditions of elders	15:1-20	7:1-23	—	—
Third Period — Galilean Ministry				
Journey to Tyre and Sidon:				
Healing of Syrophenician's daughter	15:21-28	7:24-30	—	—
Return by way of Decapolis:				
Multitudes healed	15:29-31	—	—	—
Healing of a man deaf and stuttering	—	7:31-37	—	—
Feeding of the four thousand	15:32-38	8:1-9	—	—
Pharisees and Sadducees demand a sign	15:39-16:12	8:10-21	—	—
Healing of a blind man	—	8:22-26	—	—
Journey to Caesarea Philippi:				
Peter's confession concerning Christ	16:13-20	8:27-30	9:18-21	—
Jesus' first foretelling of his death and resurrection	16:21-28	8:31-9:1	9:22-27	—
The Transfiguration	17:1-13	9:2-13	9:28-36	—
Healing of an epileptic boy	17:14-21	9:14-29	9:37-43	—
In Galilee:				
Jesus' second foretelling of his death and resurrection	17:22-23	9:30-32	9:43-45	—
Coin in the fish's mouth	17:24-27	—	—	—
Discourse: humility and forgiveness	18:1-35	9:33-50	9:46-50	—
Parable of the unmerciful servant	18:23-25	—	—	—

JESUS' THREE-YEAR MINISTRY
THE GOSPEL RECORD OF JESUS' MINISTRY (Cont.)

	Matthew	Mark	Luke	John
In Jerusalem at Feast of Tabernacles				7:1-13
Teaching in the Temple				7:14-8:2
Healing of woman taken in adultery				8:3-11
Discourse: Christ the light of the world				8:12-30
Discourse: spiritual freedom				8:31-59
Healing of a man born blind				9:1-41
Discourse: the good shepherd				10:1-21
In Jerusalem at Feast of Dedication				10:22-42
Accusation of blasphemy				
Last Few Months — Peraean Ministry				
Final departure from Galilee to Peraea	19:1-2	10:1	9:51-56	
Priority of discipleship	8:19-22		9:57-62	
The Seventy appointed and sent out			10:1-24	
Parable of the good Samaritan			10:25-37	
Visit to Mary and Martha at Bethany			10:38-42	
Jesus teaches his disciples to pray			11:1-13	
Parable of overly persistent and demanding friend			11:5-8	
Discourse: denunciation of Pharisees			11:15-54	
Discourse: trust in God's care, watchfulness for Christ's coming			12:1-59	
Parable of the rich fool			12:16-21	
Parable of the watchful servants			12:35-38	
Parable of the goodman of the house			12:39-40	
Parable of the faithful and faithless stewards			12:42-48	
Importance of repenting			13:1-5	
Parable of the barren fig tree			13:6-9	
Healing of woman bowed together 18 years			13:10-17	
Who shall be saved?			13:22-30	
Jesus' reproof of Herod and Jerusalem			13:31-35	
At dinner in chief Pharisee's house:				
Healing of a man with dropsy			14:1-6	

JESUS' THREE-YEAR MINISTRY
THE GOSPEL RECORD OF JESUS' MINISTRY (Cont.)

	Matthew	Mark	Luke	John
Parable of the wedding guest	—	—	14:7-11	—
Virtue of hospitality to the poor	—	—	14:12-14	—
Parable of the great supper	—	—	14:15-24	—
Three requirements for discipleship	—	—	14:25-27	—
Cost of discipleship — forsaking all	—	—	14:28-35	—
Parable of the lost sheep	—	—	15:1-7	—
Parable of the piece of silver	—	—	15:8-10	—
Parable of the prodigal son	—	—	15:11-32	—
Parable of unjust steward	—	—	16:1-7	—
Parable of rich man and Lazarus	—	—	16:19-31	—
Teaching on forgiveness, faith, service	—	—	17:1-10	—
Parable of the unprofitable servant	—	—	17:7-10	—
Raising of Lazarus at Bethany	—	—	—	11:1-46
Sanhedrin's plot to kill Jesus	—	—	—	11:47-53
Jesus' withdrawal to Ephraim, through the borders of Samaria and Galilee to Peraea	—	—	17:11	11:54
Healing of ten lepers	—	—	17:12-19	—
Discourse: coming of the kingdom of God and of the Son of man	—	—	17:20-18:8	—
Parable — lesson on persistence	—	—	18:1-8	—
Parable of Pharisee and publican	—	—	18:9-14	—
Concerning divorce and marriage	19:3-12	10:2-12	—	—
Blessing little children	19:13-15	10:13-16	18:15-17	—
Instructions to a rich young ruler	19:16-22	10:17-31	18:18-30	—
Dangers of wealth, rewards of selfless service	19:23-30	—	—	—
Parable of laborers in the vineyard	20:1-16	—	—	—
Jesus' third prediction of his death and resurrection	20:17-19	10:32-34	18:31-34	—
James and John want reward without labor	20:20-28	10:35-45	—	—
Healing of a blind beggar (or of two men)	20:29-34	10:46-52	18:35-43	—
Healing of Zacchaeus at Jericho	—	—	19:1-10	—
Parable of the ten pieces of money	—	—	19:11-28	—
Jesus' enemies lie in wait for him	—	—	—	11:55-57
Anointing of Jesus by Mary of Bethany	26:6-13	14:3-9	—	12:1-11

111

JESUS AS HEALER

CONTENTS:

- Research Questions
- Focus on One Healing
- Jesus' Healing Work

MATERIALS:

- Bible
- Bible Concordance

MEMORY VERSE:

"Heal the sick, cleanse the lepers, raise the dead, cast out devils: freely ye have received, freely give."

Matthew 10:8

JESUS AS HEALER
RESEARCH QUESTIONS

Directions: Research and answer the following questions. The answers can be found by using a Bible concordance or the Teacher's Notes on Jesus' Three-Year Ministry.

In order to impress upon the students this important aspect of Jesus' mission, we recommend reading some of the healings out loud from the Gospels as you find them. The impact Jesus made on his world is still felt in our world today because he told us — "... He that believeth on me, the works that I do shall he do also; ..." (John 14:12).

1. Name ten physical healings Jesus performs. In what Gospel do you find them? Where do they occur?

   a. _____   f. _____

   b. _____   g. _____

   c. _____   h. _____

   d. _____   i. _____

   e. _____   j. _____

2. Find in the Gospels where it is recorded that Jesus raises someone from the dead. Where does it happen? Locate each place on the map.

   a. _____

   b. _____

   c. _____

   d. _____

3. Name two healings of sin that Jesus performs. What are the circumstances? Give the Bible references.

   a. _____

   b. _____

JESUS AS HEALER
RESEARCH QUESTIONS (Cont.)

4. Find the one time Jesus calls a disease by name.

_____

5. Name the two instances Jesus heals someone at a distance.

a. _____

b. _____

6. Find in the Gospels where Jesus commissions his disciples to heal.

_____

7. Name ten commands or imperatives Jesus gives when he demands participation from the one being healed.

a. _____   f. _____

b. _____   g. _____

c. _____   h. _____

d. _____   i. _____

e. _____   j. _____

8. Find what healing is in all four Gospels.

_____

9. What healings does Jesus perform on non-Jews? Under what circumstances do they occur?

a. _____

b. _____

c. _____

JESUS AS HEALER
RESEARCH QUESTIONS (Cont.)

10. How many times does Jesus heal on the sabbath? Name them.

a. _____

b. _____

c. _____

d. _____

e. _____

f. _____

g. _____

11. Some healings are recorded in two or three of the Gospels. Find the healings that are unique to each one of the Gospels and are not repeated in any other.

a. _____

b. _____

c. _____

d. _____

e. _____

f. _____

g. _____

h. _____

JESUS AS HEALER
ANSWERS TO RESEARCH QUESTIONS

1. Leprosy — Matt. 8:1-4, Galilee
   Paralysis — Mark 2:1-12, Capernaum — Peter's house
   Unclean spirit — Luke 4:31-37, Capernaum synagogue
   Hemorrhaging — Mark 5:25-34, Capernaum
   Epilepsy — Mark 9:14-29, Galilee
   Demoniac — Mark 5:1-20, Decapolis
   Deafness and stuttering — Mark 7:31-37, Galilee
   Blindness — Mark 8:22-25, Bethsaida
   Vexed with a devil — Matt. 15:21-28, Syrophenician woman's daughter
   Crippled man — John 5:1-15, pool of Bethesda, Jerusalem

2. Jairus' daughter — Capernaum
   Widow's son at Nain
   Lazarus at Bethany
   Jesus at Jerusalem

3. Woman taken in adultery, John 8:3-11
   Woman who washes Jesus' feet with her tears, Luke 7:36-50

4. Gadarene demoniac, "Legion," Luke 8:26-39

5. Nobleman's son, John 4:46-54
   Centurion's servant, Matt. 8:5-13

6. Matt. 10:8

7. "Rise up and walk."
   "Go, wash in the pool of Siloam."
   "Go, and sin no more."
   "Damsel, I say unto thee, Arise."
   "Be not afraid, believe only."
   "Go thy way, Thy faith hath made thee whole."
   "Stretch forth thine hand."
   "Lazarus, come forth."

JESUS AS HEALER
ANSWERS TO RESEARCH QUESTIONS (Cont.)

8. Feeding of five thousand

9. Syrophenician's daughter
   Gadarene
   Centurion's servant

10. Seven healings: withered hand, unclean spirit, a few sick folk, spirit of infirmity, dropsy, cripple, blind man

11. Zacchaeus
    Man at the pool of Bethesda
    Nobleman's son
    Man blind and dumb
    Man deaf and stuttering
    Two blind men
    Woman bowed together
    Blind man
    Man born blind
    Man with dropsy
    Ten lepers
    Penitent sinner
    Adulterous woman
    Raising of widow's son
    Raising of Lazarus
    Malchus' ear

JESUS AS HEALER
FOCUS ON ONE HEALING

Directions: Choose one of the healings in the Gospel you are reading aloud and answer the following questions together. Have on hand some research books to delve deeper into the circumstances surrounding that healing. Teachers of younger children may want to do research on their own, gathering historical information in order to add interesting insights.

BIBLE HEALING: _____

SCRIPTURAL TEXT: _____

1. What is the problem to be healed? Where does it occur?

_____

_____

_____

2. In the healing account, does the author indicate what might be in the "patient's" thought? Can you explain those qualities?

_____

_____

_____

3. What about the environment in which the healing takes place? Is there any resistance evident from the account? Why and from whom?

_____

_____

_____

JESUS AS HEALER
FOCUS ON ONE HEALING (Cont.)

4. What rituals, traditions or customs does Jesus break (if any)?

_____

_____

_____

5. From the Gospel record, can you determine what is in Jesus' thought either from his questions or statements as he confronts the challenge?

_____

_____

_____

_____

6. What specifically does Jesus say or do in order to bring about the healing?

_____

_____

_____

_____

JESUS AS HEALER
IN-DEPTH RESEARCH OF TWO HEALINGS

Mark 1:40-45 — Healing of a leper
Leprosy was considered incurable in those days. Lepers were total outcasts. The Jewish law stated that no one could touch a leper. A leper in public had to walk around shouting, "Unclean, unclean," and even ring a bell to let others know he was approaching, according to the Torah. There was fear of contagion. Leprosy was also a physically revolting sight to any onlooker.

Verse 40: The patient came to Jesus. ". . . there came a leper . . . beseeching him, . . ."

Patient's thought: "If thou wilt, thou canst make me clean." The leper had a sense of expectancy, faith, hope, trust, humility, acknowledgment of Jesus' healing power.

Verse 41: Jesus' thought: compassion, love. "Jesus, moved with compassion, . . ." He was not afraid of touching the leper's disease: he ". . . put forth his hand, and touched him . . ." and said, ". . . be thou clean." Jesus had no hesitation in breaking that rabbinical law. Could Jesus' touch be the first human touch that individual had had in years?

Verse 42: The result? ". . . immediately the leprosy departed . . . and he was cleansed."

Mark 3:1-5 — Man with withered hand
According to rabbinical law, no one could work on the sabbath, yet here is Jesus in the synagogue again on the sabbath and being confronted by a man with a withered hand. Luke tells us it was his right hand.

In the *Gospel of Hebrews* quoted by Jerome, the man describes himself: "I was a mason seeking a livelihood with my hands: I pray thee Jesus to restore thee mine health that I may not beg meanly for my food."

Verse 2: The audience is watching — waiting to accuse Jesus.

Look at Jesus' priority over the order of service — indicating that one of the divine purposes of church is healing. He speaks to the man, "Stand forth."

JESUS AS HEALER
IN-DEPTH RESEARCH OF TWO HEALINGS (Cont.)

Verse 4: But there appears to be an obstacle to the healing from the crowd sitting there waiting to accuse Jesus. So an issue is raised by Jesus. He doesn't address the man but the audience: "Is it lawful to do good on the sabbath days, or to do evil? to save life, or to kill?" According to Jesus' theology (since he healed many times on the sabbath), the lawful thing to do is to heal. So healing must be good; leaving the man diseased must be evil. These are not dogmatic statements made by the Master Teacher. He simply asks a question.

What's the crowd's reaction? "They held their peace." In Greek, "They were silent."

Verse 5: Jesus tells the man, "Stretch forth thine hand." In other words, the man must do something—exercise the dominion which God gave him. If someone else does it for him, it is not the man's dominion but the healer's. The result of the man's obedience? ". . . his hand was restored whole as the other."

Now the crowds want to figure out a way to destroy Jesus, whose only purpose is to fulfill God's law.

JESUS AS HEALER
HEALING WORK OF JESUS

Nobleman's son — John 4:46-54

Man with unclean spirit — Mark 1:21-28; Luke 4:31-37

Peter's wife's mother — Matt. 8:14-15; Mark 1:29-31; Luke 4:38-39

Leper — Matt. 8:2-4; Mark 1:40-45; Luke 5:12-14

Man with withered hand — Matt. 12:9-13; Mark 3:1-5; Luke 6:6-10

Centurion's servant — Matt. 8:5-13; Luke 7:1-20

The paralytic — Matt. 9:2-8; Mark 2:3-12; Luke 5:17-26

Man at pool of Bethesda who couldn't walk — John 5:1-16

Man blind and dumb — Matt. 12:22-29

Dumb demoniac — Matt. 9:32-34; Luke 11:14

Man deaf and stuttering — Mark 7:32-37

Gadarene demoniac — Matt. 8:28-34; Mark 5:1-20; Luke 8:26-39

Woman — issue of blood — Matt. 9:20-22; Mark 5:25-34; Luke 8:43-48

Two blind men — Matt. 9:27-31

Daughter of Syrophenician woman — Matt. 15:21-28; Mark 7:24-30

Epileptic boy — Matt. 17:14-21; Mark 9:14-29; Luke 9:38-43

Woman "bowed together" — Luke 13:10-17

Blind man — Mark 8:22-26

Man with dropsy — Luke 14:1-6

Man born blind — John 9:1-41

Ten lepers — Luke 17:11-19

Blind beggar Bartimaeus — Mark 10:46-52; Luke 18:35-43

Malchus' ear — Luke 22:49-51

Penitent sinner — Luke 7:36-50

Zacchaeus — Luke 19:1-10

Adulterous woman — John 8:2-11

Raising of widow's son — Luke 7:11-16

Raising of Jairus' daughter — Matt. 9:18-26; Mark 5:22-43; Luke 8:41-56

Raising of Lazarus — John 11:1-46, 53

Jesus' resurrection — Matt. 28:1-10; Mark 16:1-11; Luke 24:1-12;
                      John 20:1-18; Acts 1:3

JESUS' TREATMENT
OF WOMEN

CONTENTS:

- Research Questions
- Social Position of Women
- Book List

MATERIALS:

- Bible
- Research Books

MEMORY VERSE: "And when Jesus saw her, he . . . said unto her, Woman, thou art loosed from thine infirmity. And he laid his hands on her: and immediately she was made straight, and glorified God."

Luke 13:12-13

JESUS' TREATMENT OF WOMEN
RESEARCH QUESTIONS

Directions: Research and answer the following questions.

1. How are women perceived in Jesus' time by Jewish laws and traditions?

_____

_____

_____

2. What stereotypes of womanhood does Jesus disregard?

_____

_____

_____

3. Does Jesus' treatment of women conflict with Jewish laws and traditions? Be specific in your answer.

_____

_____

_____

_____

4. How does Jesus elevate the rights of women in the society of his time as well as our time?

_____

_____

_____

_____

_____

JESUS' TREATMENT OF WOMEN
RESEARCH QUESTIONS (Cont.)

5. How does Jesus' treatment of womanhood help us today in the healing of abuse toward women in general?

_____

_____

_____

_____

6. Name the healings performed by Jesus which involve women. Under what circumstances do the healings occur?

_____

_____

_____

_____

7. Find every encounter Jesus has with women other than the healings.

_____

_____

_____

_____

8. Were there any women disciples? Can you find where they are mentioned in the Gospels?

_____

_____

_____

JESUS' TREATMENT OF WOMEN
RESEARCH QUESTIONS (Cont.)

9. How important are women as witnesses to the resurrection? Explain the circumstances and how women are involved.

_____

_____

_____

_____

10. Can you find in the Bible any prophecies pointing to womanhood's hour?

_____

_____

_____

11. Where do you find the virgin birth in prophecy? If the virgin birth had been a controversial subject when Matthew wrote his Gospel, do you think he would have included it in his narrative as his initial Scriptural authority for the birth of Jesus? Explain.

_____

_____

_____

_____

_____

JESUS' TREATMENT OF WOMEN
TOPICS FOR FURTHER STUDY

There are many instances or illustrations given by Jesus in his teachings showing the complementary roles of male and female. It appears important for Jesus to reveal the balance, equality, and parallel between the two. For example:

> Matt. 12:41 — male
> Matt. 12:42 — female
>
> Luke 15:4 — male
> Luke 15:8 — female

We have discovered nine examples in the New Testament. Can you find these and more?

MALE	FEMALE

JESUS' TREATMENT OF WOMEN
BACKGROUND INFORMATION

Almost every time Jesus broke new ground in his ministry, a woman was cast in a primary role at his side. Ten occasions can be singled out: a sick woman; a Samaritan; an adulteress; a generous woman; a penniless widow; Mary, the mother of Jesus; Mary of Magdala; a woman cured of possession by the devils; Mary and Martha (sisters of Lazarus); Claudia Procula, wife of Pontius Pilate.

Jesus initiated his public ministry at a wedding feast. The implication: woman's special responsibility to bring the spiritual element into the marriage partnership.

In healings of women, Jesus showed his belief in the spiritual equality of man and woman.

Samaritan Woman
Since Samaritans had been forced to intermarry with the Assyrians who had invaded their country, no Jew was to have further dealings with the Samaritans, yet Jesus talked to the Samaritan woman at the well. Jesus told her he is the Messiah. She was an outcast, very inferior, a foreigner, one of scanty morals and — most unthinkable of all — a woman!

". . . Jesus breached the seven hundred-year-old wall of prejudice and racial arrogance that the Jews had built to isolate Samaria" *(Jesus and Woman,* p. 44-45). Jesus was speaking to someone considered unworthy to hear such a message and incapable of understanding what he said.

When Jesus told her about worshipping God "in spirit and in truth" (see John 4:23), and that the time had come ". . . when ye shall neither in this mountain, nor yet at Jerusalem, . . . " (John 4:21), Jesus was making a direct attack on the religious structure supporting the self-serving power of a priesthood that claimed to have exclusive, divinely-granted control over man's access to his God" *(Jesus and Woman,* p. 47-48).

JESUS' TREATMENT OF WOMEN
BACKGROUND INFORMATION (Cont.)

Adulterous Woman

She was faced with being stoned to death for breaking the seventh commandment. The self-righteous Pharisee asked the question to force Jesus into defying the law of Moses — thus attempting to trap him:

> "... Moses and the law commanded us, that such should be
> stoned: but what sayest thou?" (John 8:5)

Jesus' response, "... He that is without sin among you, let him first cast a stone at her" (John 8:7), forced the crowd to leave. Now Jesus was left alone with the woman. He didn't condemn her, but told her to go and sin no more. He made it clear that the burden of sin falls on both man and woman. In Lev. 20:10, the law reads:

> "... the adulterer and the adulteress shall surely be put
> to death."

But in Jesus' time, the man, it appears, was allowed to escape punishment. The woman was dragged before the crowd as a sex object in order to degrade her. Yet Jesus treated her as a human being — with compassion (*Jesus and Woman*, p. 53).

The crowd's emotions were hatred, anger, impatience, self-righteousness, wanting to assert their superiority as males. Jesus changed the mood from hatred into reasonableness, vindictiveness into compassion and love, arrogance into forgiveness.

Mary and Martha

In Jesus' day it was frowned upon for women to give precedence to the activity of the mind over activity of the hands. Women were not supposed to have an intellect. Yet, Jesus reprimanded Martha and supported Mary's desire to listen to him. Mary set aside her chores to do this.

JESUS' TREATMENT OF WOMEN
BACKGROUND INFORMATION (Cont.)

Raising the Dead

Jesus raised the dead, and all four resurrections are closely related to women:

1) Jairus' twelve-year-old daughter

2) Widow's son at Nain

3) At the raising of Lazarus, Jesus told Martha, Lazarus' sister, that he is the resurrection and the life

4) At Jesus' resurrection he chose a woman to bear witness to the male disciples about it.

Society in Jesus' time was guided by sex barriers designed to safeguard the superiority of the male.

"Woman, being chattel, could not bear witness in a court of law or in any other place" (op. cit., p. 106). Yet Jesus told Mary of Magdala to bear witness to his resurrection.

Widow's Mite

Women were not obliged to go to the Temple or to make an offering. The widow, of her own free will, gave all she had. Value was never measured by its material worth but by the motivation prompting the gift, and the greatest motivation was love.

JESUS' TREATMENT OF WOMEN
SOCIAL POSITION OF WOMEN

A woman's principal function was wife and mother. She was subordinate to her father and then to her husband. The word "wife" means "woman belonging to a man" (*The Interpreter's Dictionary of the Bible*, Vol. 4, p. 865). The stereotype of womanhood in Jesus' day was that she was considered inferior to the male. Her husband could freely divorce her. She was required to give him unquestioning obedience. Marriage occurred between the ages of 12 and 14.

If a wife had no children, her position was very tenuous. Ridicule, scorn, humiliation were felt by any wife who was barren. Bitter sorrow would accompany her and reproach from God was inevitable, according to Jewish tradition. Young women were taught to love their husbands and children. They were taught to be sensible, chaste, kind, and submissive to husbands. They were also to learn household duties.

According to Hebrew law, both the adulterer and adulteress were to be put to death.

A daughter was less desirable than a son, so according to Hebrew law, she could be sold by the father — even sold into prostitution. The husband owned his wife and children, which gave him authority to sell his daughters into slavery or arrange their marriages.

A male was not to be alone with a woman, to look at a married woman, or to give her a greeting. It was preferable for the woman not to go out at all. Her face was to be hidden by a veil so her features would not be recognizable and thus avoid the sight of men.

In crowds, women were frowned upon, ignored, ostracized — in other words, considered only a possession or object.

One injunction stated, "Speak not much with a woman," (*Biblical Affirmations of Woman*, p. 156). Some rabbinic sayings about women express another negative attitude: "When a boy comes into the world, peace comes into the world. When a girl comes, nothing comes" (op. cit., p. 157).

JESUS' TREATMENT OF WOMEN
SOCIAL POSITION OF WOMEN (Cont.)

Women could go no further than the Court of the Gentiles and the Court of Women in the Temple. Women could participate in the synagogue service, but barriers of lattice separated the women's section from the men's. Later a gallery was built with a special entrance. Women were forbidden to teach.

A woman had no right to bear witness in a court because she was considered a liar. She always had to be backed up with a male witness. She was barred from appearing in court.

She was not supposed to think deeply or intellectually; she was considered too emotional.

In Jesus' time, many questioned whether women had a soul. Male Jews have uttered a prayer of thanksgiving, thanking God for three things: "Praised be God that he has not created me a gentile; praised be God that he has not created me a woman; praised be God that he has not created me an ignorant man" (op. cit., p. 155).

RECOMMENDED READING

All the Women of the Bible by Edith Deen
Biblical Affirmations of Woman by Leonard Swidler
Getting Better Acquainted with Your Bible by Berenice Shotwell
Jerusalem in the Time of Jesus by Joachim Jeremias
Jesus and Woman by Lisa Sergio
Sketches of Jewish Social Life in the Days of Christ by Alfred Edersheim
The Interpreter's Dictionary of the Bible, Supplementary Volume
The Land and People Jesus Knew by J. Robert Teringo
Woman in the World of Jesus by Evelyn and Frank Stagg
Women and the Genesis of Christianity by Ben Witherington III

JESUS AS TEACHER

CONTENTS:

- Research Questions
- Galilee Curriculum
- Sermon on the Mount Study
- Extended Study Topics

MATERIALS:

- Bible
- Bible Concordance
- Bible Dictionary

MEMORY VERSE:

"Blessed are the pure in heart: for they shall see God."

Matthew 5:8

JESUS AS TEACHER
RESEARCH QUESTIONS

Directions: Use a Bible concordance or the Teacher's Notes at the end of this Lesson Packet to answer the following questions.

1. Where is the kingdom of heaven or kingdom of God according to Jesus?

   _____

2. Consider the parables as symbols of the qualities which constitute the kingdom of heaven. List eight of these parables, then list the qualities you feel might be associated with each one.

   a. _____ e. _____

   b. _____ f. _____

   c. _____ g. _____

   d. _____ h. _____

3. List twelve titles or names for Jesus.

   a. _____ e. _____ i. _____

   b. _____ f. _____ j. _____

   c. _____ g. _____ k. _____

   d. _____ h. _____ l. _____

4. Find ten instructions in the Sermon on the Mount (Matt. 5-7) on how to treat other people.

   a. _____ f. _____

   b. _____ g. _____

   c. _____ h. _____

   d. _____ i. _____

   e. _____ j. _____

JESUS AS TEACHER
RESEARCH QUESTIONS (Cont.)

5. Why does Jesus speak in parables? _____

_____

_____

6. List Jesus' parables other than those defining the kingdom of heaven.

a. _____ p. _____

b. _____ q. _____

c. _____ r. _____

d. _____ s. _____

e. _____ t. _____

f. _____ u. _____

g. _____ v. _____

h. _____ w. _____

i. _____ x. _____

j. _____ y. _____

k. _____ z. _____

l. _____ aa. _____

m. _____ bb. _____

n. _____ cc. _____

o. _____ dd. _____

JESUS AS TEACHER
RESEARCH QUESTIONS (Cont.)

7. Find three instances which show how Jesus treats children.

a. _____

b. _____

c. _____

8. Find where the Gospels mention two important Jewish festival holidays. Name them.

a. _____

b. _____

9. List five different examples where Jesus overcomes natural or physical laws.

a. _____

b. _____

c. _____

d. _____

e. _____

10. Find three different instances in which Jesus breaks rabbinical law.

a. _____

b. _____

c. _____

11. Find six Bible occupations.

a. _____ c. _____ e. _____

b. _____ d. _____ f. _____

JESUS AS TEACHER
RESEARCH QUESTIONS (Cont.)

12. What is Jesus' definition of error? (see Matt. 22:29)

_____

13. What is Jesus' definition of Satan or the devil? (see John 8:44)

_____

14. From the following verses, find Jesus' description of prayer. How would you summarize his description?

Matt. 5:44 _____

Matt. 6:9-13 _____

Matt. 6:4 _____

Matt. 6:5 _____

Matt. 6:7 _____

Matt. 7:7 _____

Matt. 26:41 _____

Mark 11:24 _____

Mark 11:25 _____

Luke 18:10-14 _____

Luke 22:40 _____

Luke 22:44 _____

JESUS AS TEACHER
RESEARCH QUESTIONS (Cont.)

15. Consider the following verses and discover the nature of Jesus' prayer — when he prayed, where, how, and why. Do these examples help us to understand something of Jesus' inner thoughts and life? If so, is this what is meant by the expression, "mind of Christ," as used by Paul? (see I Cor. 2:16; Phil. 2:5)

Matt 11: 25; John 11:41 _____

Matt 14:23 _____

Matt 26:36, 39, 42, 44 _____

Mark 1:35 _____

Mark 6:46 _____

Luke 3:21 _____

Luke 5:16 _____

Luke 6:12 _____

Luke 9:18, 28-29 _____

Luke 11:1 _____

Luke 22:32, 41, 44 _____

John 11:41 _____

John 14:16 _____

John 17 (entire chapter) _____

_____

_____

_____

_____

JESUS AS TEACHER
THE GALILEE CURRICULUM

The School of Galilee: The idea for Jesus' Galilee curriculum was first introduced to us by B. Cobbey Crisler, Bible scholar and lecturer. His insight and research into the Master Teacher's lessons on subjects of interest to mankind today are not only enlightening but practical. Mr. Crisler showed us what can be found when one looks beyond a literal or surface reading of the Bible texts and discovers the possibilities of Jesus' true intent.

At least 40 subjects have been found in the Gospel narratives. Most of the lessons were taught in the Galilee area. Jesus' students were then impelled to put into practice what they had been learning — as is required by the original Greek meaning of the word "disciple."

Remember that these subjects were Jesus' definitions and may not always coincide with modern-day definitions we have known, heard, or believed.

Examples:

Race Relations — See Luke 17:12

Hygiene — See Luke 11:39

Accident Prevention — See Luke 13:3, 5

JESUS AS TEACHER
THE GALILEE CURRICULUM (Cont.)

Activity 1

Directions: List the subject (found in the Word Bank) which corresponds to the event or statement in each box below. Answers are found on page 155.

WORD BANK:

military science	pediatrics	botany
acoustics	cardiology	architecture
psychology	law	chemistry

Changing water into wine	Love your enemies . . .	Building on rock or sand

1. _____ 2. _____ 3. _____

Out of the heart proceed evil thoughts . . . Where your treasure is, there will your heart be also	Take heed therefore how ye hear	Repent ye . . .

4. _____ 5. _____ 6. _____

Sower's seed — falling on way side, thorny and good ground	Become as little children	Woe unto you lawyers . . .

7. _____ 8. _____ 9. _____

JESUS AS TEACHER
THE GALILEE CURRICULUM (Cont.)

Activity 2

Directions: Find Bible verses to correspond with these curriculum courses.

1. Hygiene	2. Etiquette	3. Light
4. Meteorology	5. Criminology	6. Theology
7. Evolution	8. Physics	9 Communication
10. Economics	11. Aeronautics	12. Biology

JESUS AS TEACHER
THE GALILEE CURRICULUM (Cont.)
Activity 2

13.   History   14.   Philosophy   15.   Banking

16.   Dietetics   17.   Surgery   18. Animal Husbandry

19. Social Relations   20. Labor Relations   21.   Agriculture

JESUS AS TEACHER
THE GALILEE CURRICULUM (Cont.)

Activity 3

BIBLE VERSE MATCHING GAME

1. _____ Repent ye . . .

2. _____ Blessed are the poor in spirit . . .

3. _____ Blessed are they that mourn . . .

4. _____ Blessed are the meek . . .

5. _____ Blessed are they which do hunger and thirst after righteousness . . .

6. _____ Blessed are the merciful . . .

7. _____ Blessed are the pure in heart . . .

8. _____ Blessed are the peacemakers . . .

9. _____ Blessed are they which are persecuted for righteousness' sake . . .

10. _____ Be ye therefore perfect . . .

11. _____ And forgive us our debts . . .

12. _____ Heal the sick, cleanse the lepers, raise the dead, cast out devils . . .

13. _____ If ye have faith as a grain of mustard seed, ye shall say unto this mountain, Remove hence to yonder place; and it shall remove;

14. _____ Except ye be converted, and become as little children . . .

15. _____ With God . . .

a. even as your Father which is in heaven is perfect.

b. for they shall be filled.

c. all things are possible.

d. for theirs is the kingdom of heaven.

e. for theirs is the kingdom of heaven.

f. for they shall inherit the earth.

g. ye shall not enter into the kingdom of heaven.

h. for they shall be comforted.

i. for they shall see God.

j. freely ye have received, freely give.

k. for the kingdom of heaven is at hand.

l. as we forgive our debtors.

m. for they shall be called the children of God.

n. for they shall obtain mercy.

o. and nothing shall be impossible unto you.

JESUS AS TEACHER
SERMON ON THE MOUNT STUDY SHEET

Directions: The following are some suggestions for deeper study of the Sermon on the Mount:

1. Compare Matthew's version (Matt. 5-7) with Luke's (Luke 6:20-49).
2. Read Matthew 5-7 in another Bible translation — Moffatt's, J. B. Phillips, *The Revised English Bible, New Jerusalem Bible, Twenty-six Translations of the New Testament*, etc.
3. Look up the verses in Bible commentaries — Dummelow's, Peake's, Abingdon, Barnes' Notes, etc.
4. Read *The Sermon on the Mount* by Joachim Jeremias (Fortress Press).
5. Look up these verses in *The Anchor Bible* on Matthew — Vol. 26 or Luke — Vol. 28.
6. Find rules and rewards of many verses.
   Example: (Rule) "Be pure in heart . . ."
   (Reward) ". . . Ye shall see God."
7. Study the concept and symbolism of candlestick (Matt. 5:15).
8. Read *The Sermon on the Mount* by W. D. Davies (Cambridge University Press).
9. Study the concept of *abba* as Jesus uses the term. *The Prayers of Jesus* by Joachim Jeremias is a helpful resource.
10. Memorize the Beatitudes (Matt. 5:3-12).
11. What questions does Jesus ask in his Sermon on the Mount? What are the eternal lessons implied in those questions?

A statement by Clement of Alexandria (A.D. 150-220) in his book, *The Rich Man's Salvation* supports the "discovery" method:
". . . *as we are clearly aware that the Saviour teaches His people nothing in a merely human way, but everything by a divine . . . wisdom, we must not understand His words literally, but with due inquiry and intelligence we must search out and master their hidden meaning*" (p. 281, 283).

JESUS AS TEACHER
SERMON ON THE MOUNT STUDY SHEET (Cont.)

12. Does the Sermon on the Mount complete the Law of Sinai or the Ten Commandments? In other words, does Jesus' fulfill the Mosaic Law or do his teachings and life disregard it?

13. Find specific verses where Jesus' teachings in this discourse show a definite split with Judaism — Pharisaism in particular. Are there verses in which Jesus upholds the roots of Judaism?

14. What are the requirements to see the kingdom of heaven within each of us? Are these impossible ideals to achieve or can we fulfill these demands on a daily basis?

15. Jesus first tells us how not to pray before he tells us how to pray. What specifically are we to do and not do in our efforts to pray?

16. What statements can be found where Jesus refers to himself?

17. What does Jesus have to say on the following subjects?

relationships	judging
prayer	true communication
behavior in regard to an enemy	law suits
fasting	treasure
forgiveness	worry, anxiety
divorce	broad way
law of retaliation	narrow way

18. Can you find in Jesus' life where he lived the teachings of the Sermon on the Mount?

19. Look up key words in the original Greek: kingdom; blessed; heaven; adversary; love; closet; glory; hypocrite.

TOPICS FOR FURTHER STUDY

• Read the Four Gospels and compare likenesses and differences. For example, compare what audience they are addressing, the story of Jesus' birth, the Passion week, etc.

• Read the first few chapters in Eusebius' *Ecclesiastical History* (Vol. I). Locate on a map of the Roman world where "tradition" says the disciples ended their lives.

• Find reference books where you can study the Bible texts in their original Greek form. (Example: *The Diaglott,* or any Greek transliteration from Greek to English.)

• Use the "Search the Scriptures" cassette tape series by B. Cobbey Crisler. Set up one hour daily with quiet time to listen and take notes. Keep the notes in a 3-ring notebook for future Bible reference and study. (These tapes can be ordered from Infinite Discovery, Inc., 1-800-475-7308.)

• Research Herod's palaces: Masada, Caesarea Maritima, Herodium, Jericho.

• Study the Roman Caesars at the time of Jesus and see what influence they had over the affairs in Palestine: Augustus, 27 B.C.-A.D. 14; Tiberius, A.D. 14-37.

• Study the Herod family and their influence on the affairs of Palestine.

• Research new archaeological finds through books found in the bibliography at the back of this book or in the *Biblical Archaeology Review* magazine.

• Read *The Gospel of Thomas* and compare it with the Gospels of Matthew, Mark, Luke, and John.

• Take one parable of Jesus and research it in one or more of the following ways:

> • in another Bible translation
>
> • in *The Anchor Bible*
>
> • analyze symbols using a Bible dictionary or word dictionary
>
> • find resource books written about Jesus' parables

• Find every instruction Jesus gives to his disciples and make a list with Bible references.

JESUS AS TEACHER
TOPICS FOR FURTHER STUDY (Cont.)

• Give as many examples as you can find where Jesus puts into practice what he preaches.

• List all the qualifications of the "Comforter" as Jesus defines it in Chapters 14, 15, and 16 of the Gospel of John.

• Read Clement of Alexandria's *The Rich Man's Salvation*. Find similarities between the Gospels and his writings.

• Using a Bible concordance, find where Jesus uses the words, "It is written."

• Did Jesus think he was the equivalent of God? Validate your answer with specific references from the Gospels. Consider how many times he speaks of God as his Father and of himself as Son. List the references.

• What is the difference between the "Son of man" and the "Son of God" as Jesus uses the terms?

• Paul tells us, "Let this mind be in you, which was also in Christ Jesus:" (Phil. 2:5). Make a list of Bible texts that would define the mind of Christ. We have found at least 31 qualities.

Examples:

> forgiveness — Luke 7:48
> singleness — Luke 11:34
> glorifies God — John 17:1, 4

JESUS AS TEACHER
ANSWERS TO RESEARCH QUESTIONS

1. Luke 17:21 — ". . . the kingdom of God is within you."

2. a. Man sowing good seed in his field — Matt. 13:24
   b. Grain of mustard seed — Matt. 13:31
   c. Leaven — Matt. 13:33
   d. Treasure hid in a field — Matt. 13:44
   e. Merchant man seeking goodly pearls — Matt. 13:45
   f. Net — Matt. 13:47
   g. Man who is a householder bringeth forth out of his treasure things new and old — Matt. 13:52
   h. Certain king which would take account of his servants — Matt. 18:23
   i. Householder going to hire laborers — Matt. 20:1
   j. Certain king which made a marriage for his son — Matt. 22:2
   k. Ten virgins — Matt. 25:1
   l. Man traveling into a far country — Matt. 25:14

3. Alpha and omega — Rev. 1:8; 22:13
   Anointed — Ps. 2:2; 45:7
   Beginning of the creation of God — Rev. 3:14
   Branch — Isa. 11:1; Zech. 3:8; 6:12
   Bridegroom — Matt. 9:15
   Brightness of the Father's glory — Heb. 1:3
   Chosen — Matt. 12:18
   Christ — Matt. 1:16; 2:4
   Cornerstone — Eph. 2:20; I Pet. 2:6
   Door of the sheep — John 10:7
   Express image — Heb. 1:3
   Faithful witness — Rev. 1:5; 3:14; 19:11
   First begotten of the dead — Rev. 1:5
   Firstborn from the dead — Col. 1:18
   Heir of all things — Heb. 1:2
   Image of the invisible God — II Cor. 4:4; Col. 1:15
   Immanuel — Isa. 7:14; Matt. 1:23
   Lamb of God — John 1:29, 36
   Lion of the tribe of Juda — Rev. 5:5
   Master — Matt. 10:24; 23:10

JESUS AS TEACHER
ANSWERS TO RESEARCH QUESTIONS (Cont.)

Mediator — I Tim. 2:5
Messiah — John 1:41
Morning star — Rev. 2:28; 22:16
Offspring of David — Rev. 22:16
Physician — Matt. 9:12
Prince of Peace — Isa. 9:6
Prophet — Deut. 18:15; Luke 24:19
Redeemer — Isa. 59:20
Resurrection and the life — John 11:25
Rock — I Cor. 10:4
Root of David — Rev. 5:5
Saviour — Luke 2:11
Servant — Isa. 42:1, 19; 44:21
Shepherd — John 10:11
Son (only begotten) — John 1:14, 18; 3:16, 18
Son of God — Matt. 4:3; 8:29; Luke 1:35
Son of man — Matt. 8:20; John 1:51
True vine — John 15:1
Way — John 14:6
Witness — Isa. 55:4

4. a. Judge not.
   b. Forgive men their trespasses.
   c. Reconcile thyself to thy brother.
   d. Be not angry with thy brother.
   e. Whosoever smites thee on the right cheek, turn to him the other also.
   f. Love your enemies.
   g. Bless them that curse you.
   h. Do good to them that hate you.
   i. Pray for them which persecute you and use you.
   j. Whatsoever ye would that men should do to you, do ye even so to them.

5. Matt. 13:10-17, 35

6. House built on rock and sand — Matt. 7:24-27
   Sower and seed — Matt. 13:3-9; 18-23
   Natural growth of the seed — Mark 4:26-29

JESUS AS TEACHER
ANSWERS TO RESEARCH QUESTIONS (Cont.)

The wicked husbandmen — Mark 12:1-11
The budding fig tree — Matt. 24:32-33
Watchful servants — Mark 13:34-37
The children in the marketplace — Matt. 11:16-19
What defiles a man — Matt. 15:10-20
The lost sheep — Luke 15:3-7
The two sons — Matt 21:28-32
The great supper — Luke 14:16-24
The two debtors — Luke 7:41-43
The good Samaritan — Luke 10:25-37
The rich fool — Luke 12:16-21
The fruitless fig tree — Luke 13:6-9
Choosing the chief rooms — Luke 14:7-11
The tower-builder and a king planning a campaign — Luke 14:28-32
The ten pounds — Luke 19:11-26
Faithful and faithless stewards — Luke 12:41-48
Blind leading the blind — Luke 6:39-42
New and old garment — Luke 5:36-39
New wine in old bottles — Luke 5:37-39
The lost drachma — Luke 15:8-10
The prodigal son — Luke 15:11-32
The unjust steward — Luke 16:1-8
Rich man and Lazarus — Luke 16:19-31
The servant's reward — Luke 17:7-10
The unjust judge — Luke 18:1-8
The Pharisee and publican — Luke 18:9-14
The door of the sheep — John 10:1-10

7. a. Tells us we must become as little children in order to enter the kingdom of heaven
   b. Raises Jairus' twelve-year-old daughter from the dead
   c. Raises the widow's son

8. a. Feast of Passover
   b. Feast of the Dedication

JESUS AS TEACHER
ANSWERS TO RESEARCH QUESTIONS (Cont.)

9. a. Walks over the water
  b. His boat is immediately at the other side of lake.
  c. Walks through closed doors after resurrection
  d. Feeds 5,000 men plus women and children with five loaves and two fish
  e. Turns water into wine

10. a. Touches a leper
  b. Touches a dead body
  c. Says he is the Son of God
  d. Heals on the sabbath
  e. Tells women to bear witness to his resurrection
  f. Talks to woman of Samaria
  g. Eats with publicans and sinners

11.

baker	merchant	scribe
basket-weaver	miner	sculptor
butcher	moneychanger	shepherd
carpenter	mourner	silversmith
centurion	musician	steward
dancer	nailmaker	stonecutter
farmer	olive tree cultivator	tailor
fisherman	physician	tanner
goldsmith	potter	tax collector
innkeeper	priest	tending goats
lawyer	procurator	tent maker
maids	quarryman	
mason	sandal-maker	

12. Not knowing the Scriptures — "Ye do err, not knowing the scriptures, nor the power of God" (Matt. 22:29).

13. Murderer from the beginning
Liar
Parable: enemy who sowed the tares
That which takes the Word out of our hearts

JESUS AS TEACHER
ANSWERS TO RESEARCH QUESTIONS (Cont.)

14. Pray for them who use you and persecute you
    Lord's Prayer
    Pray in secret
    Do not pray as the hypocrites do
    Enter into thy closet, shut the door, pray to God in secret
    Use not vain repetitions
    Ask, seek, knock
    Pray that ye enter not into temptation
    Desire is prayer; believe and ye shall receive
    Forgive, if ye have ought against any
    Pray with humility
    When in agony, pray more earnestly

15. Gratitude
    Goes up into a mountain apart to pray and was there alone
    Gethsemane — prays alone, ". . . not as I will, but as thou wilt."
    Prays the second time — "thy will be done."
    Prays the third time — "thy will be done."
    Arising a great while before day, he goes out to a solitary place
    Departs to a mountain to pray
    Prays at his baptism
    Goes into the wilderness to pray
    Continues all night in prayer
    Prays alone; takes Peter, James, and John up into a mountain to pray;
        his face is transfigured
    Prays in a certain place — then gives the Lord's Prayer
    Prays for Peter that his faith fails not
    Being in agony, he prays more earnestly
    At raising of Lazarus — gratitude
    Prays to God to send another Comforter
    Prays that God glorifies His Son; prays for the apostles and all believers
    Prays that we be with Jesus where he is

JESUS AS TEACHER

ANSWERS TO RESEARCH QUESTIONS (Cont.)

Activity 1:

1. Chemistry
2. Military Service
3. Architecture
4. Cardiology
5. Acoustics
6. Psychology
7. Botany
8. Pediatrics
9. Law

Activity 2:

1. Luke 11:39
2. Luke 10:7
3. Luke 11:35
4. Matt. 8:24; 16:1-3
5. Matt. 5:21-22
6. Matt. 4:23
7. Luke 9:16
8. Mark 6:4; John 6:19
9. Matt. 5:37
10. Matt. 6:25, 31
11. Mark 9:33-35
12. Matt. 13:31
13. John 8:58
14. Matt. 5-7
15. Matt. 25:14-29
16. Matt. 15:11
17. Luke 22:50-51
18. Luke 18:22
19. Matt. 18:21
20. Matt. 11:28, 30
21. Matt. 9:37

Activity 3:

1. — k.
2. — d.
3. — h.
4. — f.
5. — b.
6. — n.
7. — i.
8. — m.
9. — e.
10. — a.
11. — l.
12. — j.
13. — o.
14. — g.
15. — c.

JESUS AS PROPHET/ FULFILLMENT OF PROPHECY

CONTENTS:

- **Messiah's Name/Nature**
- **Messianic Prophesies**
- **Research Questions**
- **Comparisons**
  Jesus and Moses
  10 Commandments and
  Sermon on the Mount

MATERIALS:

- **Bible**

MEMORY VERSE:

". . . by a prophet the Lord brought Israel out of Egypt, and by a prophet was he preserved."

Hosea 12:13

JESUS AS PROPHET
THE MESSIAH'S NAME AND NATURE — PROPHECY AND FULFILLMENT

Directions: Look up the following Bible verses in both the Old and New Testaments. Write the name and/or nature of the verses' description in the center of the chart. Answers are on page 174.

OLD TESTAMENT	NAME	NEW TESTAMENT
Ezek. 34:23		Matt. 9:36; John 10:11; Heb 13:20
Ps. 2:2		Luke 4:18; John 1:41
Ps. 2:7		Matt. 3:17; John 10:36
Isa. 7:14		Matt. 1:23
Deut. 18:15, 18		John 6:14
Dan. 7:13		Matt. 16:13; Mark 10:45
Isa. 7:15; Isa. 53:9		Heb. 1:9
Isa. 9:2		John 8:12
Ps. 40:8		Matt. 26:39
Isa. 9:6		Acts 5:31; Rev. 1:5
Ps. 110:4		Heb. 6:20

JESUS AS PROPHET
MESSIANIC PROPHECIES FULFILLED

Directions: Look up the Bible verses in both the Old and New Testaments. Write a brief description in the center chart which describes the event or place where prophecy and fulfillment coincide. (Answers on pages 175-179.)

OLD TESTAMENT		NEW TESTAMENT
Gen. 49:10		Luke 3:33 (Matt. 1:2-3)
Dan. 9:25		Luke 2:1-2 (John 1:41)
Mic. 5:2		Matt. 2:1 (Luke 2:4)
Isa. 7:14		Matt. 1:18 (Luke 1:26-35)
Isa. 49:7; Isa. 60:3		Matt. 2:1-2
Isa. 60:6		Matt. 2:11
Hos. 11:1		Matt. 2:13-14
Jer. 31:15		Matt. 2:16
Isa. 9:1		Matt. 4:12-13

MESSIANIC PROPHECIES FULFILLED (Cont.)

OLD TESTAMENT		NEW TESTAMENT
Isa. 61:1; Mal. 4:2		Matt. 4:23 (Matt. 11:4-5)
Ps. 118:22; Isa. 53:3		John 1:11 (John 5:43; Luke 4:29; 17:25; 23:18)
Ps. 69:4 (Ps. 35:19; 109:3)		John 15:23-25
Isa. 53:3 (Ps. 69:20)		Matt. 26:36-37
Isa. 53:3		Mark 9:12
Isa. 53:4, 12		Matt. 8:16-17
Zech. 9:9; Ps. 118:26		Matt. 21:1-2, 9 (John 12: 13-14)
Ps. 41:9		Matt. 26: 21, 23
Zech. 11:12		Matt. 26:14-15
Ps. 55:12-13		Matt. 26:50

JESUS AS PROPHET
MESSIANIC PROPHECIES FULFILLED (Cont.)

OLD TESTAMENT		NEW TESTAMENT
Zech. 11:13		Matt. 27:6-7
Zech. 13:7		Matt. 26: 31, 56
Ps. 27:12 (Ps. 35:11)		Matt. 26:59
Isa. 53:7		Matt.26:62-63 (Matt. 27:12-14)
Isa. 50:6; Mic. 5:1; Isa. 53:8		Matt. 26:67 (Matt. 27:30)
Isa. 53:8		John 18:28 (Matt. 27:27)
Isa. 53:5 (See also NEB)		John 19:1
Isa. 42:3		Matt. 27:29
Ps. 69:19		Matt. 27:28
Ps. 69:21		Matt. 27:34 (John 19:29)

JESUS AS PROPHET
MESSIANIC PROPHECIES FULFILLED (Cont.)

OLD TESTAMENT		NEW TESTAMENT
Ps. 22:18		Matt. 27:35 (John 19:24)
Isa. 53:12 (Ps. 22:16)		Matt. 27:38
Ps. 22:16 Zech. 10:4; 13:6		Luke 24:39-40 (John 20:27)
Ps. 109:4; (Isa. 53:12)		Luke 23:34
Ps. 22:7-8, 13; 35:16		Matt. 27:39-43 (Mark 15:31)
Zech. 14:6-7; Amos 8:9		Matt. 27:45
Ps. 22:1		Matt. 27:46
Ps. 31:5		Luke 23:46
Ps. 34:20 (Ex. 12:46)		John 19:33, 36
Isa. 53:5; Zech. 12:10		John 19:34

JESUS AS PROPHET
MESSIANIC PROPHECIES FULFILLED (Cont.)

OLD TESTAMENT		NEW TESTAMENT
Ps. 38:11		Matt. 27:55 (John 19:25)
Isa. 53:9		Matt. 27:57-60
Isa. 53:10; Hos. 6:2; Ps. 49:15; Ps. 16:10		Mark 16:6
Ps. 68:18		Luke 24:50-51

JESUS AS PROPHET
RESEARCH QUESTIONS

Directions: Research and answer the following questions.
(Answers on pages 192-194)

1. Jesus indicates he is a prophet by the following verse: ". . . take heed: behold I have foretold you all things" (Mark 13:23). What does he predict will happen during his own lifetime and afterwards? (Example: crucifixion, resurrection, betrayal, desertion, the Comforter, etc.)

_____ _____

_____ _____

_____ _____

_____ _____

_____ _____

_____ _____

_____ _____

_____ _____

_____ _____

2. How does Jesus define his mission?

On the next page, look up the Bible verses in the center column, then write a description of Jesus' mission in your own words in the left-hand column and give an example in the right-hand column of how Jesus fulfills this mission in his life.

JESUS AS PROPHET
RESEARCH QUESTIONS (Cont.)

In your own words	Bible verse	How Jesus fulfills this mission
	Matt. 5:17	
	John 3:17	
	John 5:46	
	John 8:12; 9:5; 12:46	
	John 9:39	
	John 10:10	
	John 10:11	

JESUS AS PROPHET
RESEARCH QUESTIONS (Cont.)

In your own words	Bible verse	How Jesus fulfills this mission
	John 12:49	
	Luke 4:16-21	
	Luke 9:56	
	Luke 19:10	
	Matt. 20:28; Luke 22:27	
	Matt. 10:34	
	John 4:34	

JESUS AS PROPHET
RESEARCH QUESTIONS (Cont.)

In your own words	Bible verse	How Jesus fulfills this mission
	Matt. 15:24	
	Matt. 3:11-12; Mal. 3:2-3	

3. How often does Jesus acknowledge he is the Messiah or Christ? Under what circumstances? Why are there not many public announcements by Jesus as to who he is?

_____   _____

_____   _____

_____   _____

_____   _____

4. Why didn't the Jews recognize Jesus as fulfillment of Old Testament prophecies concerning the Messiah?

Fill in the following chart. Notice how the Jewish expectations do not coincide with Jesus' definition of the Messiah. What prevents the Jews from seeing the Messiah's true mission? As one high school student summarized this answer: "The Jews were expecting a lion, but God gave them a lamb." (Answers on pages 195-196.)

JESUS AS PROPHET
RESEARCH QUESTIONS (Cont.)

JEWISH EXPECTATION The Messiah is to:	JESUS' FULFILLMENT How does Jesus act contrary to their expectations?
defeat the enemies of Israel — bring independence from Rome	
be a warrior	
be a judge	
be a king (not a servant)	
be a conqueror (not a sufferer)	
be a political leader and re-establish the Davidic kingdom	
uphold the traditions and integrity of Judaism; only God can forgive sins	
uphold the sabbath	
uphold strict observance of the law	
reconcile the people to God	
introduce a period of spiritual and physical bliss—one of material prosperity	
be a teacher of the Torah (In the Jewish expectations, there was no evidence that they were accustomed to speak of the Messiah as the Son of God.)	

JESUS AS PROPHET
RESEARCH QUESTIONS (Cont.)

JEWISH EXPECTATION	JESUS' FULFILLMENT
	How does Jesus act contrary
The Messiah is to:	to their expectations?

restore on a higher level the unity of a national life which had been broken during the Exile	

JESUS AS PROPHET
COMPARISON OF JESUS' AND MOSES' LIVES

Directions: Before you answer the following questions, fill in the charts on the following pages. This activity illustrates the continuity between the Old and New Testaments.

1. Did Jesus see himself as the fulfillment of Moses' prophecy? (see Deut. 18:15) How?

_____

_____

_____

_____

2. Did the Jews find comparisons between events in Moses' life and Jesus' life? Give examples from the Gospels.

_____

_____

_____

_____

3. Why is it important to see the relationship between Moses and Jesus?

_____

_____

_____

_____

JESUS AS PROPHET
COMPARISON OF JESUS' AND MOSES' LIVES

Moses' Prophecy of Jesus: Deut. 18:15		Jesus' Acknowledgment of Moses' Prediction: John 5:46-47	
Scriptural Citation	Events in Moses' Life	Scriptural Citation	Events in Jesus' Life
Ex. 1:22		Matt. 2:16	
Ex. 2:6		Matt. 2:12	
Ex. 2:11-15		Phil. 2:6-8	
Deut. 18:13		Matt. 5:48	
Deut. 6:4-5		Mark 12:29	
Lev. 19:18		Mark 12:31	
Num. 16:28		John 5:30, 36-37	
Num. 12:10-15		Luke 17:12-19; Mark 1:40-45	
Ex. 16:3-4, 15		John 6:1-14	
Ex. 17:6		John 4:10-14	

JESUS AS PROPHET
COMPARISON OF JESUS' AND MOSES' LIVES (Cont.)

Scriptural Citation	Events in Moses' Life	Scriptural Citation	Events in Jesus' Life
Deut. 4:29		Matt. 6:33	
Deut. 4:39		Matt. 6:9	
Deut. 6:16		Matt. 4:7	
Ex. 13:3		Gal. 5:1	
Deut. 8:3		Matt. 4:4	
Ex. 31:18		Luke 11:20	
Ex. 34:29		Luke 9:29	
Deut. 34:6		Acts 1:9	
Num. 16:3		John 9:29; 7:15; 10:33; 10:24	
Deut. 18:18		John 12:49-50	
Deut. 18:15		John 1:45; John 5:46-47; Luke 24:44	

JESUS AS PROPHET

COMPARISON OF TEN COMMANDMENTS AND SERMON ON THE MOUNT

Directions: Find the relationship between Jesus' teachings, the Sermon on the Mount, and the Ten Commandments. How does Jesus summarize the Ten Commandments? (see Matthew 22:37-39)

Scriptural Citation	Commandments	Scriptural Citation	Sermon on the Mount
Ex. 20:3	#1	Matt. 6:9 Mark 12:29*	
Ex. 20:4-6	#2	Matt. 6:24	
Ex. 20:7	#3	Matt. 5:34; Matt. 6:9	
Ex. 20:8	#4	Mark 2:27;* Luke 13:14 *	
Ex. 20:12	#5	Matt. 12:50; * Eph. 6:1-2*	
Ex. 20:13	#6	Matt.5:21-22	
Ex. 20:14	#7	Matt.5:27-28	
Ex. 20:15	#8	Matt. 5:42; Matt. 7:12	
Ex. 20:16	#9	Matt. 7:1-5	
Ex. 20:17	#10	Matt. 5:6; Matt. 6:19; Matt. 6:33-34	

* Not in Sermon on the Mount

JESUS AS PROPHET
THE MESSIAH'S NAME AND NATURE — PROPHECY AND FULFILLMENT

OLD TESTAMENT	NAME	NEW TESTAMENT
Ezek. 34:23	shepherd	Matt. 9:36; John 10:11; Heb 13:20
Ps. 2:2	anointed, Christ	Luke 4:18; John 1:41
Ps. 2:7	Son	Matt. 3:17; John 10:36
Isa. 7:14	Immanuel	Matt. 1:23
Deut. 18:15, 18	Prophet	John 6:14
Dan. 7:13	Son of man	Matt. 16:13; Mark 10:45
Isa. 7:15; Isa. 53:9	Refuses the evil, chooses the good; does no violence, no deceit	Heb. 1:9
Isa. 9:2	Great light	John 8:12
Ps. 40:8	Does God's will	Matt. 26:39
Isa. 9:6	Prince of Peace	Acts 5:31; Rev. 1:5
Ps. 110:4	Priest	Heb. 6:20

JESUS AS PROPHET
MESSIANIC PROPHECIES FULFILLED

The full text of the Bible verses included in the charts on the next five pages are found in their entirety beginning on page 180.

OLD TESTAMENT	EVENT/PLACE	NEW TESTAMENT
Gen. 49:10	Will descend from the tribe of Judah	Luke 3:33 (Matt. 1:2-3)
Dan. 9:25	Time of birth	Luke 2:1-2 (John 1:41)
Mic. 5:2	Nativity in Bethlehem	Matt. 2:1 (Luke 2:4)
Isa. 7:14	Born of a virgin	Matt. 1:18 (Luke 1:26-35)
Isa. 49:7; Isa. 60:3	Coming of the Magi	Matt. 2:1-2
Isa. 60:6	Bringing of gifts	Matt. 2:11
Hos. 11:1	Egypt	Matt. 2:13-14
Jer. 31:15	Slaughter of infants	Matt. 2:16
Isa. 9:1	Ministry in Galilee	Matt. 4:12-13

JESUS AS PROPHET
MESSIANIC PROPHECIES FULFILLED (Cont.)

OLD TESTAMENT	EVENT/PLACE	NEW TESTAMENT
Isa. 61:1; Mal. 4:2	Healing work	Matt. 4:23 (Matt. 11:4-5)
Ps. 118:22; Isa. 53:3	Rejection by Jews	John 1:11 (John 5:43; Luke 4:29; 17:25; 23:18)
Ps. 69:4 (Ps. 35:19; 109:3)	Hated without a cause	John 15:23-25
Isa. 53:3 (Ps. 69:20)	Man of sorrows	Matt. 26:36-37
Isa. 53:3	Acquainted with grief	Mark 9:12
Isa. 53:4, 12	Suffers for sins of others	Matt. 8:16-17
Zech. 9:9; Ps. 118:26	Triumphal entry	Matt. 21:1-2, 9 (John 12: 13-14)
Ps. 41:9	Betrayed by a friend	Matt. 26: 21, 23
Zech. 11:12	30 pieces of silver	Matt. 26:14-15
Ps. 55:12-13	Calls Judas "friend"	Matt. 26:50

JESUS AS PROPHET
MESSIANIC PROPHECIES FULFILLED (Cont.)

OLD TESTAMENT	EVENT / PLACE	NEW TESTAMENT
Zech. 11:13	Potter's field	Matt. 27:6-7
Zech. 13:7	Disciples flee	Matt. 26: 31, 56
Ps. 27:12 (Ps. 35:11)	False witnesses accuse him	Matt. 26:59
Isa. 53:7	Silent when accused	Matt.26:62-63 (Matt. 27:12-14)
Isa. 50:6; Mic. 5:1; Isa. 53:8	Smitten and spat upon	Matt. 26:67 (Matt. 27:30)
Isa. 53:8	Judgment hall	John 18:28 (Matt. 27:27)
Isa. 53:5 (See also NEB)	Scourging	John 19:1
Isa. 42:3	Reed in his hand	Matt. 27:29
Ps. 69:19	Shame (scarlet robe)	Matt. 27:28
Ps. 69:21	Vinegar and gall	Matt. 27:34 (John 19:29)

JESUS AS PROPHET
MESSIANIC PROPHECIES FULFILLED (Cont.)

OLD TESTAMENT	EVENT/PLACE	NEW TESTAMENT
Ps. 22:18	Parted his garments	Matt. 27:35 (John 19:24)
Isa. 53:12 (Ps. 22:16)	Crucified with sinners	Matt. 27:38
Ps. 22:16 Zech. 10:4; 13:6	Wounds in hands and feet	Luke 24:39-40 (John 20:27)
Ps. 109:4; (Isa. 53:12)	Prays for his enemies	Luke 23:34
Ps. 22:7-8, 13; 35:16	Mockery	Matt. 27:39-43 (Mark 15:31)
Zech. 14:6-7; Amos 8:9	Darkness over the land	Matt. 27:45
Ps. 22:1	Quotes the Psalms from the cross	Matt. 27:46
Ps. 31:5	Into thy hands	Luke 23:46
Ps. 34:20 (Ex. 12:46)	Not a bone to be broken	John 19:33, 36
Isa. 53:5; Zech. 12:10	His side is pierced	John 19:34

JESUS AS PROPHET
MESSIANIC PROPHECIES FULFILLED (Cont.)

OLD TESTAMENT	EVENT/PLACE	NEW TESTAMENT
Ps. 38:11	Many women afar off	Matt. 27:55 (John 19:25)
Isa. 53:9	Buried with the rich	Matt. 27:57-60
Isa. 53:10; Hos. 6:2; Ps. 49:15; Ps. 16:10	Resurrection	Mark 16:6
Ps. 68:18	Ascension	Luke 24:50-51

JESUS AS PROPHET
MESSIANIC PROPHECIES FULFILLED

Will descend from the tribe of Judah

Gen. 49:10

The sceptre shall not depart from Judah, nor a lawgiver from between his feet, until Shiloh come; and unto him shall the gathering of the people be.

Luke 3:33 (Matt. 1:2-3

Which was the son of Aminadab, which was the son of Aram, which was the son of Esrom, which was the son of Phares, which was the son of Juda.

Time of Birth

Dan. 9:25

Know therefore and understand, that from the going forth of the commandment to restore and to build Jerusalem unto the Messiah the Prince shall be seven weeks, and threescore and two weeks: the street shall be built again, and the wall, even in troublous times.

Luke 2:1-2

And it came to pass in those days, that there went out a decree from Caesar Augustus, that all the world should be taxed. (And this taxing was first made when Cyrenius was governor of Syria.)

John 1:41

. . . We have found the Messias, which is, being interpreted, the Christ.

Nativity in Bethlehem

Mic. 5:2

But thou, Bethlehem Ephratah, though thou be little among the thousands of Judah, yet out of thee shall he come forth unto me that is to be ruler in Israel; whose goings forth have been from of old, from everlasting.

Matt. 2:1 (Luke 2:4)

Now when Jesus was born in Bethlehem of Judaea in the days of Herod the king, behold, there came wise men from the east to Jerusalem.

Born of a Virgin

Isa. 7:14

Therefore the Lord himself shall give you a sign; Behold, a virgin shall conceive, and bear a son, and shall call his name Immanuel.

JESUS AS PROPHET
MESSIANIC PROPHECIES FULFILLED (Cont.)

Matt. 1:18 (Luke 1:26-35)
Now the birth of Jesus Christ was on this wise: When as his mother Mary was espoused to Joseph, before they came together, she was found with child of the Holy Ghost.

Coming of the Magi
Isa. 49:7
. . . Kings shall see and arise, princes also shall worship, because of the Lord that is faithful, and the Holy One of Israel, and he shall choose thee.
Isa. 60:3
And the Gentiles shall come to thy light, and kings to the brightness of thy rising.
Matt. 2:1-2
Now when Jesus was born in Bethlehem of Judaea, . . . behold, there came wise men from the east to Jerusalem, Saying, Where is he that is born King of the Jews? for we have seen his star in the east, and are come to worship him.

Bringing of Gifts
Isa. 60:6
. . . they shall bring gold and incense; and they shall shew forth the praises of the Lord.
Matt. 2:11
And when they were come into the house, they saw the young child with Mary his mother, and fell down, and worshipped him: and when they had opened their treasures, they presented unto him gifts; gold, and frankincense, and myrrh.

Egypt
Hos. 11:1
When Israel was a child, then I loved him, and called my son out of Egypt.
Matt. 2:13-14
. . . behold, the angel of the Lord appeareth to Joseph in a dream, saying, Arise, and take the young child and his mother, and flee into Egypt, and be thou there until I bring thee word: for Herod will seek the young child to destroy him.

JESUS AS PROPHET
MESSIANIC PROPHECIES FULFILLED (Cont.)

Slaughter of Infants

Jer. 31:15

Thus saith the Lord; A voice was heard in Ramah, lamentation, and bitter weeping; Rahel weeping for her children refused to be comforted for her children, because they were not.

Matt. 2:16

Then Herod, when he saw that he was mocked of the wise men, was exceeding wroth, and sent forth, and slew all the children that were in Bethlehem, and in all the coasts thereof, from two years old and under, according to the time which he had diligently inquired of the wise men.

Ministry in Galilee

Isa. 9:1

Nevertheless the dimness shall not be such as was in her vexation, when at the first he lightly afflicted the land of Zebulun and the land of Naphtali, and afterward did more grievously afflict her by the way of the sea, beyond Jordan, in Galilee of the nations.

Matt. 4:12-13

Now when Jesus had heard that John was cast into prison, he departed into Galilee; And leaving Nazareth, he came and dwelt in Capernaum, which is upon the sea coast, in the borders of Zabulon and Nephthalim:

Healing Work

Isa. 61:1

The Spirit of the Lord God is upon me; because the Lord hath anointed me to preach good tidings unto the meek; he hath sent me to bind up the broken-hearted, to proclaim liberty to the captives, and the opening of the prison to them that are bound;

Mal. 4:2

. . . unto you that fear my name shall the Sun of righteousness arise with healing in his wings; . . .

Matt. 4:23

And Jesus went about all Galilee, teaching in their synagogues, and preaching the gospel of the kingdom, and healing all manner of sickness and all manner of disease among the people.

JESUS AS PROPHET
MESSIANIC PROPHECIES FULFILLED (Cont.)

Matt. 11:4-5
Jesus answered and said unto them, Go and shew John again those things which ye do hear and see: The blind receive their sight, and the lame walk, the lepers are cleansed, and the deaf hear, the dead are raised up, and the poor have the gospel preached to them.

Rejection by Jews
Ps. 118:22
The stone which the builders refused is become the head stone of the corner.
Isa. 53:3
He is despised and rejected of men; . . .
John 1:11 (John 5:43; Luke 4:29; 17:25; 23:18)
He came unto his own, and his own received him not.

Hated without a Cause
Ps. 69:4 (Ps. 35:19; 109:3)
They that hate me without a cause are more than the hairs of mine head: . . .
John 15:23-25
He that hateth me hateth my Father also. . . . now have they both seen and hated both me and my Father. But this cometh to pass, that the word might be fulfilled that is written in their law, They hated me without a cause.

Man of Sorrows
Isa. 53:3 (Ps. 69:20)
He is . . . a man of sorrows, . . .
Matt. 26:36-37
Then cometh Jesus with them unto a place called Gethsemane, . . . And he took with him Peter and the two sons of Zebedee, and began to be sorrowful . . . .

Acquainted with Grief
Isa. 53:3
He is . . . acquainted with grief: . . .
Mark 9:12
. . . it is written of the Son of man, that he must suffer many things, and be set at nought.

JESUS AS PROPHET
MESSIANIC PROPHECIES FULFILLED (Cont.)

Suffers for Sins of Others

Isa. 53:4, 12

Surely he hath borne our griefs, and carried our sorrows: . . . he bare the sin of many, . . .

Matt. 8:16-17

When the even was come, they brought unto him many that were possessed with devils: and he cast out the spirits with his word, and healed all that were sick: That it might be fulfilled which was spoken by Esaias the prophet, saying, Himself took our infirmities, and bare our sicknesses.

Triumphal Entry

Zech. 9:9

Rejoice greatly, O daughter of Zion; shout, O daughter of Jerusalem: behold, thy King cometh unto thee: he is just, and having salvation; lowly and riding upon an ass, and upon a colt the foal of an ass.

Matt. 21:1-2 (John 12:14)

And when they drew nigh unto Jerusalem, . . . then sent Jesus two disciples, Saying unto them, Go into the village over against you, and straightway ye shall find an ass tied, and a colt with her: loose them, and bring them unto me.

Ps. 118:26

Blessed be he that cometh in the name of the Lord: . . .

Matt. 21:9 (John 12:13)

And the multitudes that went before, and that followed, cried, saying, Hosanna to the Son of David: Blessed is he that cometh in the name of the Lord; . . .

Betrayed by a Friend

Ps. 41:9

Yea, mine own familiar friend, in whom I trusted, which did eat of my bread, hath lifted up his heel against me.

Matt. 26:21, 23

And as they did eat, he said, Verily I say unto you, that one of you shall betray me. . . . He that dippeth his hand with me in the dish, the same shall betray me.

JESUS AS PROPHET

MESSIANIC PROPHECIES FULFILLED (Cont.)

Thirty Pieces of Silver

Zech. 11:12

And I said unto them, If ye think good, give me my price; and if not, forbear. So they weighed for my price thirty pieces of silver.

Matt. 26:14-15

Then one of the twelve, called Judas Iscariot, went unto the chief priests, And said unto them, What will ye give me, and I will deliver him unto you? And they covenanted with him for thirty pieces of silver.

Calls Judas "Friend"

Ps. 55:12-13

. . . it was not an enemy that reproached me; . . . But it was thou, a man mine equal, my guide, and mine acquaintance.

Matt. 26:50

And Jesus said unto him, Friend, wherefore art thou come? Then came they, and laid hands on Jesus, and took him.

Potter's Field

Zech. 11:13

And the Lord said unto me, Cast it unto the potter: a goodly price that I was prised at of them. And I took the thirty pieces of silver, and cast them to the potter in the house of the Lord.

Matt. 27:6-7

And the chief priests took the silver pieces, and said, It is not lawful for to put them into the treasury, because it is the price of blood. And they took counsel, and bought with them the potter's field, to bury strangers in.

The Disciples Flee

Zech. 13:7

. . . smite the shepherd, and the sheep shall be scattered: . . .

Matt. 26:31, 56

Then saith Jesus unto them, All ye shall be offended because of me this night: for it is written, I will smite the shepherd, and the sheep of the flock shall be scattered abroad . . . Then all the disciples forsook him, and fled.

JESUS AS PROPHET
MESSIANIC PROPHECIES FULFILLED (Cont.)

False Witnesses Accuse Him

Ps. 27:12 (Ps. 35:11)

Deliver me not over unto the will of mine enemies: for false witnesses are risen up against me, and such as breathe out cruelty.

Matt. 26:59

Now the chief priests, and elders, and all the council, sought false witness against Jesus, to put him to death;

Silent when Accused

Isa. 53:7

He was oppressed, and he was afflicted, yet he opened not his mouth: he is brought as a lamb to the slaughter, and as a sheep before her shearers is dumb, so he openeth not his mouth.

Matt. 26:62-63

And the high priest arose, and said unto him, Answerest thou nothing? . . . But Jesus held his peace . . .

Matt. 27:12-14

And when he was accused of the chief priests and elders, he answered nothing. Then said Pilate unto him, Hearest thou not how many things they witness against thee? And he answered him to never a word; . . .

Smitten and Spat Upon

Isa. 50:6

I gave my back to the smiters, and my cheeks to them that plucked off the hair: I hid not my face from shame and spitting.

Mic. 5:1

. . . they shall smite the judge of Israel, with a rod upon the cheek.

Isa. 53:8

. . . for the transgression of my people was he stricken.

Matt. 26:67 (Matt. 27:30)

Then did they spit in his face, and buffeted him; and others smote him with the palms of their hands.

JESUS AS PROPHET
MESSIANIC PROPHECIES FULFILLED (Cont.)

Judgment Hall

Isa. 53:8
He was taken from prison and from judgment: . . .
John 18:28 (Matt. 27:27)
Then led they Jesus from Caiaphas unto the hall of judgment: . . .

Scourging

Isa. 53:5
. . . with his stripes (scourging in NEB) we are healed.
John 19:1
Then Pilate therefore took Jesus, and scourged him.

Reed in his Hand

Isa. 42:3
A bruised reed shall he not break, . . .
Matt. 27:29
And when they had platted a crown of thorns, they put it upon his head, and a reed in his right hand: . . .

Scarlet Robe (Shame)

Ps. 69:19
Thou hast known my reproach, and my shame, . . .
Matt. 27:28
And they stripped him, and put on him a scarlet robe.

Vinegar and Gall

Ps. 69:21
They gave me also gall for my meat; and in my thirst they gave me vinegar to drink.
Matt. 27:34 (John 19:29)
They gave him vinegar to drink mingled with gall: and when he had tasted thereof, he would not drink.

JESUS AS PROPHET
MESSIANIC PROPHECIES FULFILLED (Cont.)

Parted his Garments
Ps. 22:18
They part my garments among them, and cast lots upon my vesture.
Matt. 27:35 (John 19:24)
And they crucified him, and parted his garments, casting lots:

Crucified with Sinners
Isa. 53:12 (Ps. 22:16)
. . . he was numbered with the transgressors;
Matt. 27:38
Then were there two thieves crucified with him, . . .

Wounds in the Hands and Feet
Ps. 22:16
. . . they pierced my hands and my feet.
Zech. 10:4; 13:6
Out of him came forth . . . the nail, . . . And one shall say unto him, What are these wounds in thine hands? Then he shall answer, Those with which I was wounded in the house of my friends.
Luke 24:39-40 (John 20:27)
Behold my hands and my feet, that it is I myself: . . . And when he had thus spoken, he shewed them his hands and his feet.

Prays for his Enemies
Ps. 109:4 (Isa. 53:12)
For my love they are my adversaries: but I give myself unto prayer.
Luke 23:34
Then said Jesus, Father, forgive them; for they know not what they do . . .

Mockery
Ps. 22:7-8, 13
All they that see me laugh me to scorn: they shoot out the lip, they shake the head, saying, He trusted on the Lord that he would deliver him: . . . They gaped upon me with their mouths, . . .

JESUS AS PROPHET
MESSIANIC PROPHECIES FULFILLED (Cont.)

Ps. 35:16
With hypocritical mockers . . . they gnashed upon me with their teeth.
Matt. 27:39-43 (Mark 15:31)
And they that passed by reviled him, wagging their heads, And saying, Thou
that destroyest the temple, and buildest it in three days, save thyself . . . .
Likewise also the chief priests mocking him, . . . said, He saved others;
himself he cannot save . . . He trusted in God; let him deliver him now, . . .

Darkness over the Land
Zech. 14:6-7
And it shall come to pass in that day, that the light shall not be clear, nor
dark: But it shall be one day which shall be known to the Lord, not day, nor
night: . . .
Amos 8:9
And it shall come to pass in that day, saith the Lord God, that I will cause the
sun to go down at noon, and I will darken the earth in the clear day:
Matt. 27:45
Now from the sixth hour there was darkness over all the land unto the ninth
hour.
Quotes the Psalms from the Cross
Ps. 22:1
My God, my God, why hast thou forsaken me? . . .
Matt. 27:46
And about the ninth hour Jesus cried with a loud voice, saying, Eli, Eli, lama
sabachthani? that is to say, My God, my God, why hast thou forsaken me?

Into Thy Hands
Ps. 31:5
Into thine hand I commit my spirit: . . .
Luke 23:46
And when Jesus had cried with a loud voice, he said, Father, into thy hands
I commend my spirit: and having said thus, he gave up the ghost.

JESUS AS PROPHET
MESSIANIC PROPHECIES FULFILLED (Cont.)

Not a Bone to be Broken
Ps. 34:20 (Ex. 12:46)
He keepeth all his bones: not one of them is broken.
John 19:33, 36
But when they came to Jesus, and saw that he was dead already, they brake not his legs: For these things were done, that the scripture should be fulfilled, A bone of him shall not be broken.

His Side is Pierced
Isa. 53:5
But he was wounded (pierced in NEB) for our transgressions, . . .
Zech. 12:10
. . . they shall look upon me whom they have pierced, . . .
John 19:34
But one of the soldiers with a spear pierced his side, and forthwith came there out blood and water.

Many Women afar off
Ps. 38:11
. . . my kinsmen stand afar off.
Matt. 27:55 (John 19:25)
And many women were there beholding afar off, which followed Jesus from Galilee, ministering unto him:

Buried with the Rich
Isa. 53:9
And he made his grave with the wicked, and with the rich in his death; . . .
Matt. 27:57, 58, 60
. . . there came a rich man of Arimathaea, named Joseph, . . . He went to Pilate, and begged the body of Jesus. . . . And laid it in his own new tomb, . . .

JESUS AS PROPHET
MESSIANIC PROPHECIES FULFILLED (Cont.)

Resurrection

Isa. 53:10

. . . he shall prolong his days . . .

Hos. 6:2

. . . in the third day he will raise us up, and we shall live in his sight.

Ps. 49:15; 16:10

. . . God will redeem my soul from the power of the grave:

. . . thou wilt not leave my soul in hell; . . .

Mark 16:6

. . . Be not affrighted: Ye seek Jesus of Nazareth, which was crucified: he is risen; he is not here: . . .

Ascension

Ps. 68:18

Thou hast ascended on high, . . .

Luke 24:50-51

And he led them out as far as to Bethany, . . . And it came to pass, while he blessed them, he was parted from them, and carried up into heaven.

JESUS AS PROPHET
ANSWERS TO RESEARCH QUESTIONS
(from page 164)

1. Jesus' predictions:
   - False Christs — Matt. 24:5, 24; Mark 13:6, 22
   - False prophets — Matt. 24:11
   - There will be great tribulation — Matt. 24:21
   - Nation shall rise against nation — Mark 13:8
   - Earthquakes, famines — Mark 13:8
   - Pestilences — Matt. 24:7
   - The sun will be darkened, no light from the moon — Mark 13:24
   - We shall see the Son of man coming in the clouds — Mark 13:26
   - Jesus' followers will be brought before councils, rulers, and kings; they will be beaten in the synagogues — Mark 13:9
   - Brother shall betray brother, etc. — Mark 13:12
   - Jesus' followers will be hated of all men — Matt. 10:22; Mark 13:13
   - Destruction of the temple — Matt. 24:2; Mark 13:2; Luke 19:43-44; Luke 21:5-6
   - Jesus predicts another Comforter will come — John 14:16, 26; 15:26; 16:7
   - Jesus predicts our sorrow shall be turned into joy — John 16:20
   - Jesus' prophetic hour — John 12:23
   - Woman's prophetic hour — John 16:21
   - ". . . I will see you again, . . ." — John 16:22
   - ". . . the Son of man shall come in the glory of his Father, . . . "— Matt. 16:27
   - Jesus' followers will sit in the throne of Jesus' glory, and ". . . ye also shall sit upon twelve thrones, judging the twelve tribes of Israel." — Matt. 19:28
   - " . . . the Son of man shall sit on the right hand of the power of God." — Luke 22:69
   - Heaven and earth shall pass away, but not Jesus' words — Mark 13:31
   - Peter's denial — Matt. 26:34; Mark 14:30; Luke 22:34; John 13:38
   - Betrayal — Matt. 17:22; 20:18; 26:21, 23; Mark 14:18; John 6:64
   - Desertion — Mark 14:27; John 16:32
   - The crucifixion — Matt. 16:21; 17:22-23; 20:19; Mark 8:31; 9:12; Luke 9:22; 17:25
   - The resurrection — Matt. 12:40; 16:21; 17:23; John 3:14; 12:32

JESUS AS PROPHET
ANSWERS TO RESEARCH QUESTIONS (Cont.)
(from pages 165-167)

2. Jesus' definitions of his mission:
- Matt. 5:17 — "Think not that I am come to destroy the law, or the prophets: I am not come to destroy, but to fulfil."
- John 3:17 — "For God sent not his Son into the world to condemn the world; but that the world through him might be saved."
- John 5:46 — "For had ye believed in Moses, ye would have believed me: for he wrote of me."
- John 8:12; John 9:5 — "As long as I am in the world, I am the light of the world."
- John 9:39 — ". . . Jesus said, For judgment I am come into this world, that they which see not might see; and that they which see might be made blind."
- John 10:10 — ". . . I am come that they might have life, and that they might have it more abundantly."
- John 10:11 — ". . . the good shepherd giveth his life for the sheep."
- John 12:49 — "For I have not spoken of myself; but the Father which sent me, he gave me a commandment, what I should say, and what I should speak."
- Luke 4:16-21 (quotes Isa. 61:1-2) — ". . . preach the gospel to the poor; . . . heal the brokenhearted, to preach deliverance to the captives, and recovering of sight to the blind, to set at liberty them that are bruised,"
- Luke 9:56 — "For the Son of man is not come to destroy men's lives, but to save them. . ."
- Luke 19:10 — "For the Son of man is come to seek and to save that which was lost."
- Luke 22:27 — ". . . I am among you as he that serveth."
- Matt. 10:34 — "Think not that I am come to send peace on earth: I came not to send peace, but a sword."
- John 4:34 — "Jesus saith unto them, My meat is to do the will of him that sent me, and to finish his work."
- Matt. 15:24 — ". . . I am not sent but unto the lost sheep of . . . Israel."
- Matt. 3:11-12 — "I indeed baptize you with water unto repentance: but he that cometh after me is mightier than I, whose shoes I am not worthy to bear: he shall baptize you with the Holy Ghost, and with fire:"

JESUS AS PROPHET
ANSWERS TO RESEARCH QUESTIONS (Cont.)
(from page 167)

3. Jesus' acknowledgment that he is the Messiah:
   - Matt. 16:16-17 — Peter's statement, "Thou art the Christ," and Jesus' affirmation — ". . . flesh and blood hath not revealed it unto thee, but my Father which is in heaven."
   - John 4:25-26 — Samaritan woman at the well — Jesus states, ". . . I that speak unto thee am he."
   - John 9:35-37 — After Jesus heals the man born blind, he makes the statement, ". . . Thou hast both seen him, and it is he that talketh with thee."
   - Mark 14:61-62; Luke 22:67-70 — Jesus before the high priest: "Art thou the Christ?" Jesus answers, "I am."
   - Luke 4:16-21 — Jesus quotes from Isaiah 61 and then acknowledges his fulfillment as the prophesied anointed one: ". . . This day is this scripture fulfilled . . ."
   - Luke 7:20, 22 — John the Baptist's inquiry, "Art thou he that should come?" Jesus says that his words and works reveal who he is.
   - Luke 24:27, 44 — On the night of his resurrection, Jesus goes through Moses, the prophets and the Psalms "the things concerning himself" as fulfillment of those prophecies.
   - John 3:16 — In the conversation with Nicodemus, Jesus states that God gave his only begotten Son.
   - John 10:25 — "I told you, and ye believed not: the works that I do in my Father's name, they bear witness of me."

JESUS AS PROPHET
ANSWERS TO RESEARCH QUESTIONS (Cont.)
(from pages 167-169)

JEWISH EXPECTATION The Messiah is to:	JESUS' FULFILLMENT How does Jesus act contrary to their expectations?
defeat the enemies of Israel — bring independence from Rome	Gives tribute to Caesar; a disciple is a tax collector; overthrows the tables of the moneychangers
be a warrior	"Love your enemies." — Matt. 5:44
be a judge	"I judge no man." — John 8:15
be a king (not a servant)	When the people try to make him a king, he departs to a mountain alone. — John 6:15 servant — Matt. 12:17-21; 20:28
be a conqueror (not a sufferer)	The Son of man must suffer — Mark 8:31; 9:12, 31; 10:33, 45 Jesus crucified like a criminal
be a political leader and re-establish the Davidic kingdom	"My kingdom is not of this world." — John 18:36
uphold the traditions and integrity of Judaism (only God can forgive sins)	Eats with publicans and sinners; forgives sinners — Mark 2:7-12
uphold the sabbath	Jesus heals on the sabbath; Son of man is Lord of the sabbath. His disciples pluck ears of corn on the sabbath.

JESUS AS PROPHET
ANSWERS TO RESEARCH QUESTIONS (Cont.)
(from pages 167-169)

JEWISH EXPECTATION	JESUS' FULFILLMENT
uphold strict observance of the law	Touches the lepers and dead; talks with women in public
reconcile the people to God	Jesus' prayer — his followers be with him where he is — John 17:24 Lamb of God — which taketh away the sin of the world — John 1:29
introduce a period of spiritual and physical bliss, one of material prosperity	Give to the poor. — Matt. 19:21 A rich man shall hardly enter into the kingdom of heaven. — Matt. 19:23-24
be a teacher of the Torah	"As my Father hath taught me, I speak these things." — John 8:28 not a scribe, not taught by an authorized rabbi
no evidence that they were accustomed to speak of the Messiah as the Son of God	Matt. 3:17 — "This is my beloved son . . ." Matt. 14:33 — "Thou art the Son of God." Matt. 17:5; Luke 1:35; John 6:69; John 9:35-37
restore on a higher level the unity of national life which had been broken during the Exile	"I am come to set a man at variance against his father, and the daughter against her mother, . . ." — Matt. 10:35

JESUS AS PROPHET
COMPARISON OF JESUS' AND MOSES' LIVES

Moses' Prophecy of Jesus:	Jesus' Acknowledgment:
"The Lord thy God will raise up unto thee a Prophet from the midst of thee, of thy brethren, like unto me; unto him ye shall hearken;" Deut. 18:15	*"For had ye believed Moses, ye would have believed me: for he wrote of me. But if ye believe not his writings, how shall ye believe my words?"* John 5:46-47

Scriptural Citation	Events in Moses' Life	Scriptural Citation	Events in Jesus' Life
Ex. 1:22	*Pharaoh casting sons into the river.*	Matt. 2:16	*Herod kills male babies in Bethlehem.*
Ex. 2:6	*Child taken up by daughter of Pharaoh — doesn't tell it's one of the Hebrew children.*	Matt. 2:12	*Wise men do not go back and tell Herod they've seen the Messiah.*
Ex. 2:11-15	*Moses killing an Egyptian — flees to desert. Leaves his life as a prince.*	Phil. 2:6-8	*Jesus comes in the form of a servant.*
Deut. 18:13	*Thou shalt be perfect with the Lord thy God.*	Matt. 5:48	*Be ye therefore perfect, even as your Father which is in heaven is perfect.*
Deut. 6:4-5	*Shema — one Lord — Love the Lord thy God with all thine heart. . .*	Mark 12:29	*Jesus quotes Shema as first of all the commandments.*
Lev. 19:18	*Love thy neighbour as thyself.*	Mark 12:31 John 5:30,	*Jesus quotes this as the second of all commandments.*

JESUS AS PROPHET
COMPARISON OF JESUS' AND MOSES' LIVES
(Cont.)

Scriptural Citation	Events in Moses' Life	Scriptural Citation	Events in Jesus' Life
Num. 16:28	*Moses saying — the Lord hath sent me to do all these works.*	36-37	*Jesus acknowledges he was sent by God. Also in John 6:44, 57; John 8:16, 18, 29, 42; John 12:49; John 17:25; John 20:21.*
Num. 12:10-15	*Moses heals Miriam of leprosy.*	Luke 17:12-19; Mark 1:40-45	*Jesus heals ten lepers and one leper.*
Ex. 16:3-4, 15	*Manna — feeding the children of Israel in the wilderness.*	John 6:1-14	*Feeding of 5,000 and 4,000.*
Ex. 17:6	*Water comes out of a rock for Moses.*	John 4:10-14	*Jesus giving a well of water springing up into everlasting life.*
Deut. 4:29	*Seek God — and ye shall find Him.*	Matt. 6:33	*Seek ye first the kingdom of God . . .*
Deut. 4:39	*The Lord is God in heaven above, and upon the earth beneath: there is none else.*	Matt. 6:9	*Our Father, which art in heaven, . . .*
Deut. 6:16	*Ye shall not tempt the Lord your God.*	Matt. 4:7	*Jesus quotes this during the temptation.*
Ex. 13:3	*Ye came out of the house of bondage.*	Gal. 5:1	*Be not entangled again with yoke of bondage. Christ hath made us free.*

JESUS AS PROPHET
COMPARISON OF JESUS' AND MOSES' LIVES
(Cont.)

Scriptural Citation	Events in Moses' Life	Scriptural Citation	Events in Jesus' Life
Deut. 8:3	*Man doth not live by bread alone.*	Matt. 4:4	*Jesus quotes this during the temptation.*
Ex. 31:18	*Two tables of testimony, written with the finger of God.*	Luke 11:20	*If I with the finger of God cast out devils . . .*
Ex. 34:29	*Moses' face shone while he talked with God.*	Luke 9:29	*Jesus' countenance altered during the transfiguration.*
Deut. 34:6	*Possibility that Moses ascended.*	Acts 1:9	*Jesus' ascension.*
Num. 16:3	*Questioning of Moses' divine appointment.*	John 9:29; 7:15; 10:33; 10:24	*Pharisees and Scribes question Jesus' divine appointment.*
Deut. 18:18	*Moses' acknowledgment of his divine appointment.*	John 12:49-50	*Jesus — I have not spoken of myself, but the Father which sent me.*
Deut. 18:15	*The Lord thy God will raise up unto thee a Prophet from the midst of thee, of thy brethren, like unto me; unto him shall ye hearken;*	John 5:46-47; John 1:45; Luke 24:44	*Jesus tells us that Moses wrote of him.* *Philip tells Nathanael — We have found him of whom Moses did write.* *All things must be fulfilled, which were written in the law of Moses . . . concerning me.*

JESUS AS PROPHET
COMPARISON OF TEN COMMANDMENTS AND SERMON ON THE MOUNT

Scriptural Citation	Commandments	Scriptural Citation	Sermon on the Mount
Ex. 20:3	#1 Thou shalt have no other gods before me.	Matt. 6:9; Mark 12:29 *	Our Father which art in heaven. The Lord our God is one Lord.
Ex. 20:4-6	#2 No graven images.	Matt. 6:24	No man can serve two masters.
Ex. 20:7	#3 Do not take the name of the Lord thy God in vain.	Matt. 5:34, Matt 6:9	Swear not at all. God's name should be hallowed.
Ex. 20:8	#4 Keep the sabbath day holy.	Mark 2:27;* Luke 13:14*	Sabbath was made for man. Jesus heals on the sabbath.
Ex. 20:12	#5 Honour thy father and thy mother . . .	Matt. 12:50;* Eph. 6:1-2 *	Whosoever does God's will, the same is Jesus' brother, sister, and mother.
Ex. 20:13	#6 Thou shalt not kill.	Matt. 5:21-22	Don't be angry with your brother.
Ex. 20:14	#7 Thou shalt not commit adultery.	Matt. 5:27-28	Whosoever looketh on a woman to lust after her hath committed adultery with her already in his heart.
Ex. 20:15	#8 Thou shalt not steal.	Matt. 5:42; Matt. 7:12	Give to him that asketh thee, . . . Golden Rule

JESUS AS PROPHET
COMPARISON OF TEN COMMANDMENTS
AND SERMON ON THE MOUNT (Cont.)

Scriptural Citation	Commandments	Scriptural Citation	Sermon on the Mount
Ex. 20:16	#9 Thou shalt not bear false witness against thy neighbour.	Matt. 7:1-5	Judge not . . .
Ex. 20:17	#10 Do not covet.	Matt. 5:6; Matt. 6:19; Matt. 6:33-34	Hunger and thirst after righteousness. Lay up treasures in heaven. Seek first the kingdom of God — all these things shall be added unto you.

* Not in Sermon on the Mount

THE TEMPLE AND JEWISH WORSHIP

CONTENTS:

- **Jewish Worship**
- **Religious Sects**
- **Herod's Temple**
  Events
  Illustration
  Inner Courts Map
- **Recommended Reading**

MATERIALS:

- **Bible**
- **Resource Books**

MEMORY VERSE:

". . . the hour cometh, and now is, when the true worshippers shall worship the Father in spirit and in truth: . . ."

John 4:23

The Temple and Jewish Worship
DESCRIPTION OF JEWISH WORSHIP
(See background information on pages 211-214)

TEMPLE WORSHIP IN JERUSALEM:

_____

_____

_____

_____

_____

_____

SYNAGOGUE WORSHIP:

_____

_____

_____

_____

_____

_____

FEAST OF PASSOVER:

_____

_____

_____

_____

_____

_____

The Temple and Jewish Worship
STRUCTURE OF JEWISH RELIGIOUS SECTS
(See background information on pages 215-216)

Pharisees	**Sadducees**
Sanhedrin	**Zealots**
Scribes	**Essenes**

The Temple and Jewish Worship
HEROD'S TEMPLE

Directions: Describe the following and explain what happens in each area.

1. Court of the Gentiles: _____

_____

2. Court of the Women: _____

_____

3. Court of Israel (Men's Court): _____

_____

4. Court of Priests: _____

_____

5. Altar of Burnt Offering: _____

_____

6. Laver: _____

_____

7. The Holy Place: _____

_____

8. Alms Boxes: _____

_____

9. Solomon's Porch: _____

_____

10. Gate Beautiful: _____

_____

11. Holy of Holies: _____

_____

The Temple and Jewish Worship
TEMPLE INNER COURTS MAP
(Blank)

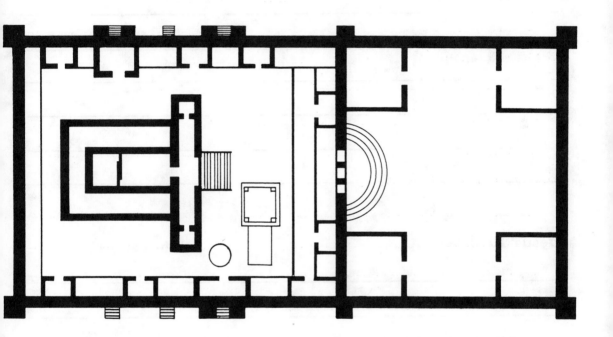

The Temple and Jewish Worship
EVENTS ASSOCIATED WITH THE TEMPLE

Directions: Describe the events which took place in and around the Temple during Jesus' ministry. (Answers found on pages 107-111)

Jesus' Sermons   **Bible Verses**

_____   _____

_____   _____

_____   _____

_____   _____

_____   _____

Jesus' Healings   **Bible Verses**

_____   _____

_____   _____

_____   _____

_____   _____

_____   _____

The Temple and Jewish Worship
EVENTS ASSOCIATED WITH THE TEMPLE (Cont.)

Specific Events (other than physical healings)   **Bible Verses**

_____   _____

_____   _____

_____   _____

_____   _____

_____   _____

_____   _____

Accusations by Jews   **Bible Verses**

_____   _____

_____   _____

_____   _____

_____   _____

_____   _____

The Temple and Jewish Worship
RECOMMENDED READING

1. **Herod's Temple.** Search for information about Herod's Temple. The following books may be helpful:

- *Getting Better Acquainted with Your Bible*, Berenice Shotwell
- *Jerusalem As Jesus Knew It*, John Wilkinson
- *Jerusalem in the Time of Jesus*, Joachim Jeremias
- *Jesus and His Times*, Reader's Digest
- "Reconstructing Herod's Temple Mount in Jerusalem," *Biblical Archaeology Review*, November/December, 1989
- *The Archaeology of the New Testament*, Jack Finegan
- *The Bible and Archaeology*, J. A. Thompson
- *The Interpreter's Dictionary of the Bible* (Vol. 4)
- *The Land and People Jesus Knew*, J. Robert Teringo
- *The Temple, Its Ministry and Services As They Were at the Time of Jesus Christ*, Alfred Edersheim
- *The Anchor Bible Dictionary*, ed. David Noel Freedman

2. **Passover.** Read together the description of the Passover celebration.

- *Jesus — The Man Who Changed History*, Meryl Doney (Lion Publishers)

The Temple and Jewish Worship
BACKGROUND INFORMATION

Temple Mount Area:

The Temple Mount area could accommodate large crowds. Herod the Great enlarged the former area by building new walls on the south, north, and west and extending the eastern wall. In today's terms, it would take five football fields to fill the area from north to south and three football fields to fill it from east to west. Hundreds of visitors — Jews and Gentiles — would travel long distances just to glimpse this wonder of the ancient Roman world. The Temple Mount area consisted of the Temple and its individual courts and was surrounded by a great courtyard.

Court of the Gentiles:

This courtyard was a large open area that surrounded the Temple complex. Jews and Gentiles could mingle in this area. Pilgrims entered the southern side of the Temple Mount through the Huldah Gates (now called the Double Gate). This Triple Gate (located further to the east of the Double Gate) was probably used by the priestly class. On the southern end of the western wall, a staircase was built (over what is now called "Robinson's Arch") which led into the Royal Stoa where the moneychangers kept their stalls. Coins bearing the image of Caesar had to be exchanged for silver shekels. In all probability, it was in here where Jesus overthrew the tables of the moneychangers. After A.D. 30, the Sanhedrin would meet at the eastern end of the Royal Stoa. The Court of the Gentiles also contained stalls where oxen, sheep, goats, doves, and pigeons were sold for sacrifice. Along the eastern side of the outer Court of the Gentiles, a magnificent colonnade was built known as "Solomon's Porch." A high retaining wall supported this platform. John 10:22-23 mentions that Jesus entered into Solomon's Porch at the Feast of the Dedication.

A short distance within the Court of Gentiles, a balustrade was inscribed with the following words: "No foreigner is to enter within the balustrade and enclosure around the temple area. Whoever is caught will have himself to blame for his death which will follow." In Ephesians 2:14, Paul makes reference to the warning.

The Temple and Jewish Worship
BACKGROUND INFORMATION (Cont.)

Court of the Women:

This Court was not for women only, but it was the farthest court in which women could enter. It was a regular place of assembly for public worship. Here women could occupy the raised gallery which surrounded the Court on three sides, most likely above the colonnades. Along the pillars of the colonnades were placed 13 trumpet-shaped **alms boxes** to receive the offerings and dues. These boxes were probably the treasury into which the widow's mites were cast (Luke 21:2). In each of the four corners of the Court were chambers: The **Chamber of Wood** where priests inspected wood for the altar; the **Chamber of Lepers** where those who had been healed of the dreaded disease would come to wash in a ritual bath for purification and then present themselves to the priests at the Gate of Nicanor; the **Chamber of Oils** which held oil and wine for the drink-offerings; the **Chamber of the Nazarites** or "consecrated ones," who could not cut their hair, could not drink wine, or approach the dead.

Court of the Israelites:

This Court was a narrow strip and raised somewhat above the Court of Women. Only male Jews could enter. Here they would hand the priests their sacrificial animal.

Court of the Priests:

This Court was located in front of and on both sides of the Sanctuary or Holy Place. Only priests were allowed in this area. The most prominent object in the area was the immense altar of animal sacrifice. The bronze laver — located southwest of the altar — was provided for the priests to wash their hands and feet. The intent of this cleansing was to make the priests holy.

Temple Edifice Proper:

The Holy Place — The first room in the Temple edifice was called "The Holy Place." It contained the seven-branched lampstand or menorah, a table for the shewbread and flagons of wine, and the altar of incense.

The Holy of Holies — The second room in the Temple edifice and was screened by a veil. In Jesus' time, it contained no furnishings at all. In Old

The Temple and Jewish Worship
BACKGROUND INFORMATION (Cont.)

Testament times, this small four-squared room contained the ark of the covenant which housed the Ten Commandments. Only the high priest could enter into the Holy of Holies one time a year on the Day of Atonement. According to Josephus, it was ". . . inaccessible and inviolable, and not to be seen by any . . ." (*The Wars of the Jews*, Book 5, page 707).

Feast of Passover:

This was a Pilgrim Festival and probably the most important of all Jewish celebrations. Thousands of priests and Levites would attend to the Temple services and sacrifices. After the unblemished lamb had been slaughtered and its blood sprinkled against the base of the altar, the individual would take the remains back to the household for the evening meal to be eaten with unleavened bread and bitter herbs. During the course of the meal, the story of the Exodus would be recited. During the entire Passover week, nothing that contained yeast could be eaten. According to the Gospels, it was during Passover that Jesus was crucified.

Synagogue:

The word "synagogue" means "congregation" or "assembly." Some scholars believe that the first synagogues were erected during the Babylonian Captivity (6th century B.C.) when Jews no longer had the Temple in which to pray and teach. Ten men could form a synagogue. A Pharisee was in charge of the services. By 70 A.D., 480 synagogues were in Jerusalem. Each one consisted of a house for reading the Law and a place where school children received their elementary instruction. All synagogues were destroyed when Rome destroyed the Temple in Jerusalem.

Services on the sabbath consisted of readings from the Scriptures — the Law and Prophets. Services always began with the *Shema*: "Hear, O Israel, the Lord our God is one Lord; and thou shalt love the Lord thy God with all thine heart, and with all thy soul, and with all thy might" (Deut. 6:4). The reading was always read in Hebrew, but most Jews during Jesus' time spoke Aramaic, so an interpreter gave a verse-by-verse explanation (a *targum*).

The furnishings in the synagogue consisted of:

— Torah shrine, where one or more Torah scrolls and probably some prophets' scrolls were kept. It was a chest (sometimes called "ark") covered

The Temple and Jewish Worship
BACKGROUND INFORMATION (Cont.)

and screened from the sight of the congregation with a veil or curtain. In the center was the *bema,* or elevated podium for reading of the lessons and benedictions.

— Stone benches, not chairs, for sitting were along the walls. Women and children sat upstairs in a separate gallery from the men.

— Menorah — the seven-branched candlestick or lampstand located in the large assembly room.

The synagogue was open three times a day for prayer. The Torah was read completely through once in three years. It was customary to invite any stranger who happened to attend the services to deliver a prophetic lesson. Ten elders chose a head of the synagogue.

How did the synagogue differ from the Temple? There were no animal sacrifices, no altar, no priests.

The Temple and Jewish Worship
STRUCTURE OF THE JEWISH RELIGIOUS SCENE

Pharisees: (approximately 6,000)
- possible meaning: "the separate ones"
- upheld tradition and Scripture
- usually middle class, artisans
- teachers and preachers of the Law (Torah — first five books of the Bible) — they were convinced they had the correct interpretation of the Law
- controlled every phase of Jewish daily life
- taught in the synagogues
- hoped for Messiah, King and Kingdom
- believed in the prophets' writings which nourished a Messianic hope
- believed in resurrection and angels and a future world
- often arrogant, pious, self-righteous, hypocritical, corrupt, spiritually dull
- plotted Jesus' death
- Paul was a Pharisee
- Nicodemus and Jairus were Pharisees
- believed in immortality of the soul
- represented the common people

Sadducees:
- believed in free choice
- from aristocratic, wealthy families
- controlled Temple worship — which was the main function of the Law
- accepted written Law (Torah) only
- rejected oral law and prophets
- denied existence of angels and spirits
- denied resurrection or any afterlife
- held power in the Sanhedrin
- hostile to Jesus' movement
- believed in animal sacrifice
- "high priest" came only from this sect
- very politically motivated
- rigid, narrow-minded, conservative
- wanted to keep the status quo
- maintained their position as long as they worked with the Romans

The Temple and Jewish Worship
STRUCTURE OF THE JEWISH RELIGIOUS SCENE (Cont.)

- chief priests belonged to this party
- the party died out with the destruction of the Temple

Scribes:
- some sat on the Sanhedrin
- their job was to study, preserve Jewish law
- copied and edited all Scripture; taught and interpreted the Law
- we owe them preservation of the Old Testament
- they were not paid; had to have another job
- most were Pharisees
- held the seat of honor in a synagogue
- represented a distinctive class in the community
- Gamaliel was a Pharisee and scribe
- professional lawyers — interrogated Jesus on certain points of the law
- they were venerated with reverential awe and respect
- their words had sovereign authority

Zealots:
- patriotic, fanatical group
- wanted to make war against Rome
- wanted a David-like king to be the Messiah
- right-wing extremists
- disciple Simon was a Zealot
- fought the Romans in A.D. 67 which caused the fall of Jerusalem
- made a last stand at Masada A.D. 73 — almost all committed suicide
- plotted Paul's death

Sanhedrin:
- means "council" in English; "a sitting together"
- supreme court for the Jews — their highest authority for 200 years
- 70 members; priests, scribes, elders
- met in Temple area; sat in semicircle for trials; sessions could be held at the residence of the high priest

The Temple and Jewish Worship
STRUCTURE OF THE JEWISH RELIGIOUS SCENE (Cont.)

- high priest presided (Roman procurator appointed and deposed the high priest; seven high priests were appointed and deposed during Herod the Great's reign)
- debated and passed judgment
- crimes they could judge: heresy, blasphemy, sabbath-breaking
- could ask for death penalty if had approval of Roman governor
- a capital case could not be tried on the eve of the sabbath or festival
- could intervene when a lower court couldn't agree on the interpretation of the Mosaic law
- responsible for taxes collected by publicans (money would go into imperial treasury)
- ceased to function in A.D. 70

Essenes: (approximately 4,000 in population)
- lived in communes; withdrew from the world
- monks; believed in purity, no marriage; gave up worldly goods
- opposed to slavery, war, animal sacrifice
- Dead Sea Scrolls discovered in 1947 in caves near Qumran possibly authored by the Essenes

The Temple and Jewish Worship
INNER COURTS MAP
(Filled-in)

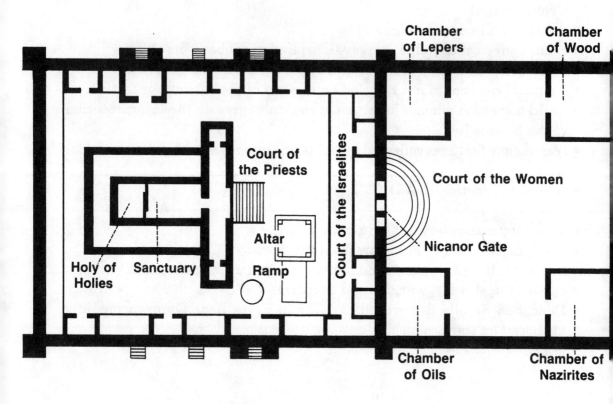

Source: Reader's Digest, *Jesus and His Times*

THE TEMPLE

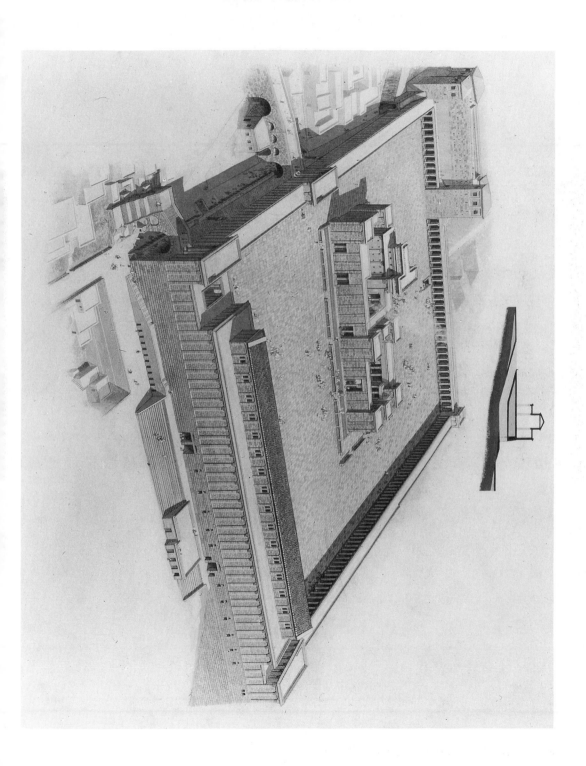

THE TEMPLE

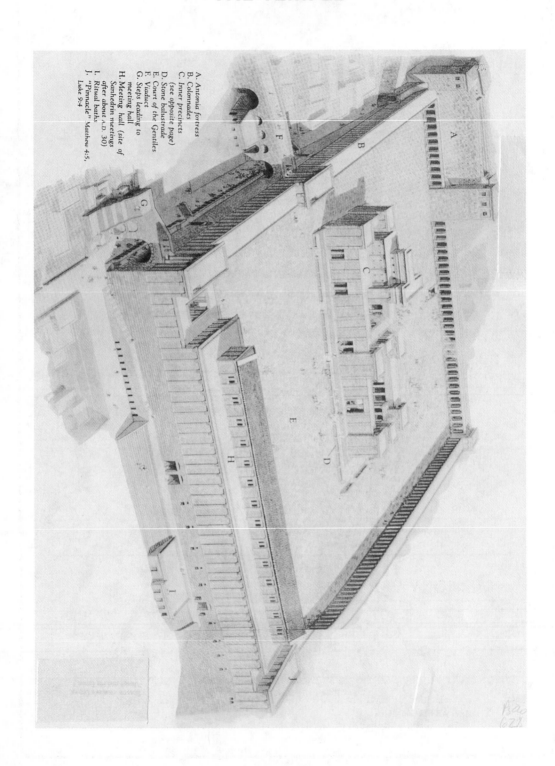

A. Antonia fortress
B. Colonnades
C. Inner precincts
   (see opposite page)
D. Stone balustrade
E. Court of the Gentiles
F. Viaduct
G. Steps leading to
   meeting hall
H. Meeting hall (site of
   Sanhedrin meetings
   after about A.D. 30)
I. Ritual baths
J. "Pinnacle" Matthew 4:5,
   Luke 9:4

THE PASSION NARRATIVE

CONTENTS:

- **Resurrection Week**
- **Research Questions**
- **Research Activities**
- **Ancient Jerusalem Map**
- **Gospel Record**
- **Walk to Emmaus**

MATERIALS:

- **Bible**
- **Resource Books**
- **Bible Concordance**

MEMORY VERSE:

". . . Father, if thou be willing, remove this cup from me: nevertheless not my will, but thine, be done."

Luke 22:42

THE PASSION NARRATIVE
RESEARCH ACTIVITIES

1. Review the Teacher's Notes for the Passover in the Temple Lesson Packet. Establish an understanding of the holiday's purpose and rituals.

2. Use the map of Jerusalem on page 230 in this section. Talk about each location. Hand out a blank map of the same area and let the students fill in as many places as they can remember.

3. Read the Passion narrative out loud from the Gospels and talk about the events that took place. Compare the record with each Gospel as to common details and differences:
   Matt. 27:27-61
   Mark 15:16-47
   Luke 23:26-56
   John 19:1-42

4. Look up individual text passages in Bible commentaries.

5. If possible, watch *Jesus of Nazareth* video — the last part about the crucifixion and resurrection.

6 Listen to the music of Handel's *Messiah*. Review the Bible verses chosen for the music.

7 Fill in the Resurrection Week Chart together on pages 224-225. Use the Teacher's Notes for reference.

THE PASSION NARRATIVE
RESEARCH ACTIVITIES (Cont.)

8. Why was Jesus crucified? _____

_____

_____

_____

9. Did the *disciples* know the crucifixion was imminent? Why or why not?

_____

10 What were the Jewish expectations of the Messiah and did they conflict with Jesus' role as fulfillment? Review pages 195-196.

_____

_____

_____

11. Why was Jesus called the "Lamb of God?" What does a lamb symbolize? Where else is the term used besides the Gospels?

_____

12. Why did Jesus allow women to be the ones to tell about the resurrection to his male disciples?

_____

_____

_____

13. How did Jesus threaten the integrity of Judaism?

_____

_____

THE PASSION NARRATIVE
ANCIENT JERUSALEM MAP
(Blank)

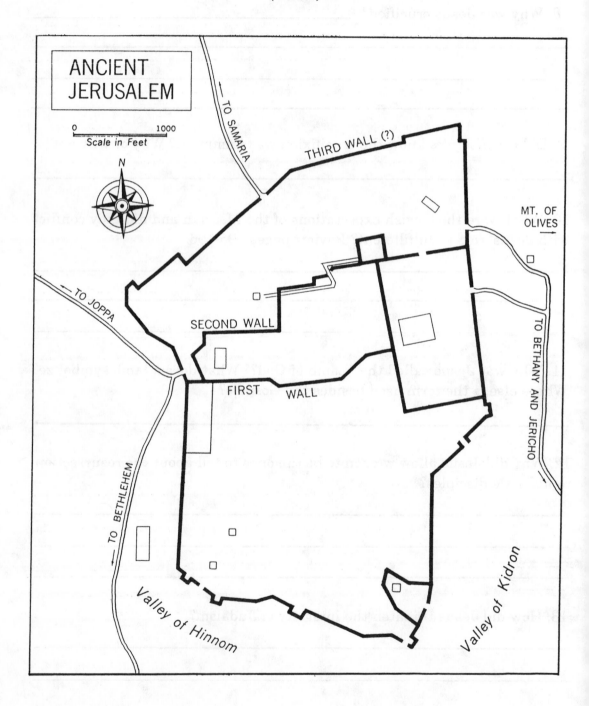

THE PASSION NARRATIVE
RESURRECTION WEEK CHART

Sunday

_____

_____

_____

_____

_____

Monday

_____

_____

_____

_____

_____

Tuesday

_____

_____

_____

_____

_____

ACTIVITY SHEET

THE PASSION NARRATIVE
RESURRECTION WEEK CHART (Cont.)

Wednesday

_____

_____

_____

_____

Thursday

_____

_____

_____

_____

Friday

_____

_____

_____

_____

Saturday _____

Sunday _____

THE PASSION NARRATIVE
RESURRECTION WEEK ANSWERS

Sunday — Palm Sunday
Triumphal entry into Jerusalem — hailed as King

Monday — Second cleansing of the Temple
Curses the barren fig tree

Tuesday — • Last day of public teaching: parables, discourses
- Foretells the destruction of the Temple
- Guest of Simon the leper (woman anoints Jesus)
- Chief priests and Judas conspire

Wednesday — The record is silent — perhaps in seclusion at Bethany

---

Thursday — Two views of Last Supper and Passover:

**SYNOPTIC GOSPELS
(MATTHEW, MARK, LUKE):**
Passover = Thursday
Last Supper = Thursday

Reason for this view: Jesus says, "I will eat the Passover . . ."
Reason against this view: A trial would not be held on Passover night

JOHN:
Passover = Friday
Last Supper = Thursday

Reason for this view: "Lamb of God" slain at same time as Passover lamb

---

THE PASSION NARRATIVE
RESURRECTION WEEK ANSWERS (Cont.)

Thursday (Cont.)
Last Supper held probably from 6:00-9:00 p.m.
- Washing disciples' feet
- Jesus names the betrayer
- Jesus institutes the Lord's Supper
- Jesus foretells Peter's denial
- Jesus prays for his disciples and the world

9:15-10:30 p.m. — Garden of Gethsemane
- Prays three times
- Disciples sleep
- Betrayed by a kiss
- Healing of Malchus' ear

11:00 p.m. — Trial before Annas
Midnight — Illegal trial before Caiaphas and a few members of the Sanhedrin; Judas commits suicide

---

Friday — 5:30 a.m. — Jesus is put before all of the Sanhedrin in order for them to ratify the charges of the night committee so he could go to Pilate as a condemned man.

Before 10:00 a.m. — Roman civil trial before Pilate — outdoors on a platform or bema; John also presents some private interviews between Jesus and Pilate inside the Antonia Fortress; Pilate sends Jesus to Herod Antipas where in Luke's version Jesus is mocked by soldiers and dressed as a king; then Herod sends Jesus back to Pilate. In Matthew's Gospel, Jesus is mocked by soldiers in the Judgment Hall, dressed as a king, spat upon, smitten, and then led away to be crucified.

Crucifixion —
Mark's Gospel states the third hour (approximately 9:00 a.m.);
John's Gospel states the sixth hour (around noon)

THE PASSION NARRATIVE
RESURRECTION WEEK ANSWERS (Cont.)

Crucifixion —
  Darkness from the sixth until the ninth hour (maybe from noon until 3:00 p.m.)

  Jesus gives up the ghost (John 19:30)

  The veil of the Temple is rent around 3:00 p.m. (In John's version, the slaughtering of the lambs would have begun around noon.)

Burial before sundown — the ninth hour before sabbath begins. In John's version — before Passover begins

---

Saturday — Sealing of the tomb

Sunday — Resurrection (women at the empty tomb)

THE PASSION NARRATIVE
ANCIENT JERUSALEM MAP
(Filled-In)

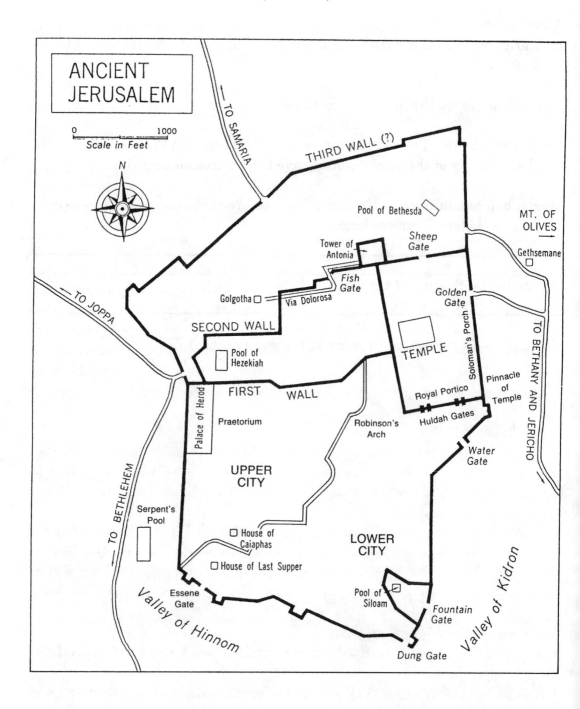

THE PASSION NARRATIVE
BACKGROUND MAP INFORMATION

Jerusalem
• 33 miles from the Mediterranean Sea, 14 miles west of north end of the Dead Sea.

Temple Mount
• Solomon's Temple was the first building here (950 B.C.). It was burned to the ground in 586 B.C. by Nebuchadnezzar, and many Jews were taken to Babylon .
• The Temple was rebuilt in 516 B.C. and desecrated in 168 B.C. by Antiochus the Great. Judas Maccabeus cleansed and restored it to use in 165 B.C.
• Herod the Great began construction on a much larger Temple in 20 B.C. to win popularity with Jews. It was not completely finished until A.D. 64 — six years before its final destruction by Rome. The Romans built a temple to Jupiter on the site. Moslems captured Jerusalem in A.D. 639 and a Mosque was built in 690. The Crusaders captured Jerusalem in 1099 and converted the Mosque to a church. One hundred years later, the Crusaders were defeated by the Arabs, and the Dome of the Rock became a sacred place to the Moslems who said it was the spot where Abraham prepared to sacrifice his son Isaac (Gen. 22:1-22) and where Mohammed is said to have been taken up into heaven.

Golden Gate
• The gate that led directly into the Temple area. According to Jewish tradition, the Messiah would enter through this gate when he came to Jerusalem (Matt. 21:8-11). Also this gate was the traditional route Jesus took to Gethsemane (Matt. 26:30).
• The Turkish governor of Jerusalem in 1530 blocked up the gate in hope of postponing the day of judgment and end of the world because the Golden Gate, says the legend, is where the trumpet will sound and the dead will be raised.

Wailing Wall or Western Wall
• A portion of Herod's wall which was built around the west side of the Temple area.
• It is called the Wailing Wall still today because early in the morning and

THE PASSION NARRATIVE
BACKGROUND MAP INFORMATION (Cont.)

late at night, the wall is covered with drops of dew which, legend says, are tears that the wall sheds while weeping with Israel in her exile. Jews still come here to bewail the loss of their Temple. Jews put bits of paper containing prayers into the cracks of the wall.

• To the left of the Western Wall is Wilson's Arch. To the right of the Western Wall is Robinson's Arch. This arch was also a royal bridge used to get to the Temple site from the upper city.

Huldah Gates and Grand Staircase

• The gates were cut into the southern wall of Herod's Temple Mount. The stairs led up to the Temple through these gates.

Saint Stephen's Gate

• This was near the place where Stephen was martyred while Saul of Tarsus looked on (Acts. 7:54-60).

Pool of Bethesda *("house of mercy")*

• According to Eusebius, this pool was used to wash sheep before sacrificing them in the Temple.

• Jesus healed a lame man by the pool (John 5:1-16).

Antonia Fortress *(named after Mark Antony)*

• Pilate's Judgment Hall — Outside its entrance is where some think Jesus was condemned. In the hall, a scarlet robe was placed on Jesus, a crown of thorns put upon his head, and a reed placed in his right hand (Matthew's version — 27:2-31).

• The fortress was built to give protection to the Temple in case of uprisings. The Roman garrison was housed here during the time of the feasts. Paul was taken here when he was rescued from the Jewish mob.

• The fortress was outside the northern city wall. Stone pavements have been found here (see John 19:13) as well as a large Roman pavement discovered under the so-called *Ecco Homo* arch. This pavement was in the courtyard of the Antonia Fortress. The pavement was designed as a parade ground for Romans and horses and for the approach to Pilate's judgment seat *(bema)*, to which Jesus was led. There are patterns scratched in the stones of

THE PASSION NARRATIVE
BACKGROUND MAP INFORMATION (Cont.)

the pavement which represent the play board for popular games that Roman soldiers played while on duty.

Herod's Palace
• It was located south of the citadel. Wise men from the East came to Jerusalem and asked Herod, "Where is he that is born King of the Jews?" (Matt. 2:1-2).
• Herod erected three towers to guard the western entrance to the city and his palace. One he named Hippicus (a friend); one, Phasael (his brother); and one, Mariamne (his favorite wife).

Kidron Valley
• It is a valley (three miles long) between Jerusalem and the Mount of Olives where the Brook Kidron runs. This river bed or wadi remains dry except during the rainy season. It was a favorite burial site.

Valley of Hinnom
• Rubbish was burned here.

Golgotha *(skull) (Calvary) (Matt. 27:33; Mark 15:22; John 19:17)*
• It was the site of the crucifixion. The crucifixion occurred outside the city walls (John 19:20). A possible location would be on a rocky hill 250 yards northeast of the Damascus Gate. The reason for its name — "Golgotha" — is that it was the Jewish place of stoning, and the rocky terrain showed the form of a skull.

Feast of Tabernacles *(Succoth) (John 7:10-52)*
• It was also known as the Feast of Booths. Pilgrims kept the feast for seven days. It represented Israel's assimilation of an ancient village festival and commemorated the wanderings in the wilderness. The ceremony consisted of offering up the golden vessel of water brought from the pool of Siloam.
• Jesus taught in the Temple during the feast.

Feast of the Dedication *(John 10:22-23)*
• An eight-day festival which was known also as Lights or Hanukkah. It

THE PASSION NARRATIVE
BACKGROUND MAP INFORMATION (Cont.)

commemorates the victories of Judas Maccabeus in 165 B.C. and the purification and rededication of the Temple under his leadership.
• It was during this feast that the Bible said, ". . . Jesus walked in the temple in Solomon's porch" (John 10:23).

Feast of Weeks *(Shauvot)*
• It was also known as the Pentecost — 50 days after the Passover. It is the end of the grain harvest and the beginning of the season for offering the first fruits.

Yom Kippur
• It is the Day of Atonement — ten days after the New Year.

Garden of Gethsemane
• The site on the Mount of Olives where Jesus "prayed more earnestly" on the night of his betrayal by Judas.

THE PASSION NARRATIVE
THE GOSPEL RECORD OF PASSION WEEK

	Matthew	Mark	Luke	John
Sunday	21:1-11	11:1-11	19:29-44	12:12-19
Triumphal entry into Jerusalem on a donkey				
Palms put in his path — people crying "Hosanna"	—	—	—	—
Monday				
Barren fig tree cursed	21:18-19	11:12-14	—	—
Second cleansing of the Temple	21:12-17	11:15-19	19:45-48	—
Monday night — Jesus probably in Bethany	—	11:11-12	—	—
Tuesday — last public day of teaching				
Fig tree withered	21:20-22	11:20-26	—	—
Questioning of Jesus' authority	21:23-27	11:27-33	20:1-8	—
Parables of warning to the nation:				
Of two sons	21:28-32	—	—	—
Of the vineyard of the wicked husbandmen	21:33-46	12:1-12	20:9-19	—
Of marriage of king's son	22:1-14	—	—	—
Three questions by Jewish parties	22:15-40	12:13-34	20:20-40	—
Jesus' irrefutable question about Christ	22:41-46	12:35-37	20:41-44	—
Discourse: denunciation of				
Pharisees and scribes — eight woes	23:1-39	12:38-40	20:45-47	—
Widow's mites	—	12:41-44	21:1-4	—
Greeks (Gentiles) seek Jesus	—	—	—	12:20-36
Rejection of Christ by the Jews	—	—	—	12:37-50
Jesus foretells destruction of the Temple	24:1-2	13:1-2	21:5-6	—
Olivet discourse: destruction of Jerusalem, signs of Christ's Coming, Last Judgment	24:3; 25:46	13:3-37	21:7-38	—
Guest of Simon the leper, woman anoints Jesus	26:6-13	14:3-9	—	—
Parables of warning to his disciples:				
Of fig tree and young leaves	24:32-33	13:28-29	21:29-31	—
Of household and porter watching	—	13:34-36	—	—
Of the ten virgins	25:1-13	—	—	—
Of the talents	25:14-30	—	—	—
Description of Last Judgment	25:31-46	—	—	—
Conspiracy of chief priests and Judas	26:1-5, 14-16	14:1-2, 10-11	22:1-6	—

THE PASSION NARRATIVE
THE GOSPEL RECORD OF PASSION WEEK (Cont.)

Event	Matthew	Mark	Luke	John
Wednesday (The record is silent — probably retirement and seclusion, maybe in Bethany.)	—	—	—	—
Thursday — 6:00-9:00 p.m. Last Supper: observance of Feast of Passover (John's version has the Passover on Friday), washing of disciples' feet, naming of betrayer, instituting of Lord's Supper, foretelling of Peter's denial	26:17-35	14:12-31	22:7-38	13-17
Discourse: Christ the way, truth, life	—	—	—	14:1-31
Discourse: the vine and the branches	—	—	—	15:1-27
Discourse: his going and returning	—	—	—	16:1-33
Jesus' prayer to God for his apostles and all believers	—	—	—	17:1-26
Thursday — 9:00-10:30 p.m. In Gethsemane, his prayer repeated three times while disciples sleep	26:30, 36-46	14:26, 32-42	22:39-46	18:1
Betrayal and arrest	26:47-56	14:43-52	22:47-53	18:2-12
Healing of Malchus' ear	—	—	22:51	—
Jewish ecclesiastical trial:				
Before Annas, father-in-law of Caiaphas — 11:00 p.m.	—	—	—	18:13-23
Before Caiaphas and Sanhedrin	26:57-75	14:53-72	22:54-65	18:24-27
Friday — early morning Peter's denial	26:69-74	14:66-72	22:55-62	18:25-27
Before Sanhedrin at daybreak	27:1-2	15:1	22:66-71	—
Judas hangs himself (cf. Acts 1:16-20)	27:3-10	—	—	—
Roman civil trial: — Before 10:00 a.m.				
Before Pilate	27:2, 11-14	15:1-5	23:1-5	18:28-38
Before Herod (Antipas)	—	—	23:6-12	—
Before Pilate	27:15-31	15:6-20	23:13-25	18:39-19:16
Crucifixion (9:00 a.m. - Mark's Gospel; Noon - John' Gospel)	27:32-56	15:21-41	23:26-49	19:17-37

THE PASSION NARRATIVE
THE GOSPEL RECORD OF PASSION WEEK (Cont.)

	Matthew	Mark	Luke	John
Seven last sayings: Luke 23:34, 43; John 19:26-27; Matt. 27:46 (Mark 15:34); John 19:28, 30; Luke 23:46				
Darkness, earthquake, veil of Temple rent — noon-3:00 p.m.	27:50-54	15:33, 38	23:44-45	—
Burial in Joseph of Arimathaea's new tomb	27:57-61	15:42-47	23:50-56	19:38-42
Saturday Sealing of tomb, guard posted	27:62-66	—	—	—
Sunday **Resurrection:** The empty tomb	28:1-8	16:1-8	24:1-8	20:1-10
The guards' report to Sanhedrin	28:11-15	—	—	—

THE PASSION NARRATIVE
FORTY DAYS FROM RESURRECTION TO ASCENSION

Directions: Find the Bible verse or verses describing Jesus' appearances to the following people. Where do the appearances take place? Is Jesus always recognized at first?

1. Mary Magdalene _____

2. The women _____

3. Two disciples on walk to Emmaus _____

4. Peter _____

5. Apostles (without Thomas) _____

6. Apostles (Thomas present) _____

7. Seven apostles at Sea of Galilee _____

8. The apostles and 500 other disciples _____

9. James _____

10. All the apostles _____

What about post-Ascension appearances?

11. Stephen _____

12. Paul — road to Damascus _____

13. John on Patmos _____

ANSWERS:

1. Mark 16:9
2. Matt. 28:9
3. Luke 24:13-34
4. I Cor. 15:5
5. John 20:19
6. Mark 16:14; John 20:26
7. John 21:4-14
8. I Cor. 15:6
9. I Cor. 15:7
10. I Cor. 15:7
11. Acts 7:55
12. I Cor. 15:8
13. Rev. 1:1, 9-19

THE PASSION NARRATIVE
WALK TO EMMAUS

PART I

Directions: Answer the following questions as you read through the verses (Luke 24:13-49).

1. Verses 18-24: How much do the disciples know when Jesus meets them?

_____

_____

2. Verses 16 and 21: Do they recognize Jesus at first? What is their

expectation?_____

_____

3. Verse 21: What is the disciples' attitude toward Jesus?

_____

_____

4. Verses 22-23: What is the rumor going around?

_____

_____

5. Verse 25: What is Jesus' rebuke to these disciples?

_____

_____

6. Verses 25-27: The disciples talk about current events. Jesus talks about

the prophets. Why? _____

_____

_____

THE PASSION NARRATIVE
WALK TO EMMAUS (Cont.)

7. Verses 25-27: What is the basis for knowing Jesus? _____

_____

_____

8. Verse 27: Who or what is teaching the disciples — the Bible or Jesus?
Explain the difference. _____

_____

_____

9. Verse 26: What have the disciples missed in Old Testament prophecies
concerning the Messiah? _____

_____

_____

_____

10. What verse indicates to the readers the beginning of the Christian
church? _____

_____

_____

_____

11. Verses 44-45: What is the key ingredient to understanding the Scriptures?

_____

_____

_____

THE PASSION NARRATIVE
WALK TO EMMAUS (Cont.)

PART II

Directions: In the book of Acts, find where Peter, Philip, Apollos, and Paul take their listeners on the "Walk to Emmaus." Write out each incident in your own words.

_____

_____

_____

_____

_____

_____

_____

_____

_____

_____

_____

_____

_____

_____

_____

THE PASSION NARRATIVE
ANSWERS TO WALK TO EMMAUS

PART I

1. They knew Jesus had been crucified, but they did not know the truth about the resurrection — only that the women found the tomb empty.
2. No, they did not recognize Jesus at first. They did not expect a suffering Messiah to be the fulfillment of prophecy.
3. The disciples felt let down by Jesus. They trusted in Jesus to be the Messiah, yet he was crucified like a criminal. To a Jew, the idea of a suffering Messiah was "monstrous."
4. The rumor was that he was alive, but no one believed the women's report. The male disciples found the empty tomb. Jesus was gone.
5. Jesus calls them "fools and slow of heart" because they did not understand the prophecy.
6. The disciples would have understood the current events taking place if they had understood prophecy.
7. The basis for knowing Jesus is to know the Scriptures.
8. The Bible is teaching them, so it's not human opinion but divine revelation revealing to them Jesus' mission as defined by the prophets.
9. They missed the part of a suffering Messiah. Had they seen this part of prophecy, they would not have scattered.
10. Verse 32: Their hearts were burning within because Jesus opened the Scriptures to them in a way they had not seen before.
11. The key is to understand prophecy.

PART II

1. Acts 2:22-41
2. Acts 3:12-26
3. Acts 7:37
4. Acts 8:26-35
5. Acts 9:1-22

6. Acts 10:38-48
7. Acts 17:2-3
8. Acts 18:24-28
9. Acts 26:22-28
10. Acts 28:23

BIBLE TEST

CONTENTS:

- Bible Test
- Bible Map Test
- Crossword Puzzle

MATERIALS:

- Bible

MEMORY VERSE:

". . . Go ye into all the world, and preach the gospel to every creature."

Mark 16:15

BIBLE TEST

PART 1

a. synagogue
b. the Temple
c. *petra*
d. Pharisee
e. prophet
f. *logos*

g. Sanhedrin
h. Gentile
i. disciple
j. Passover
k. rabbi
l. *Christos*

m. publican
n. *parakletos*
o. apostle
p. Sadducees
q. Essenes
r. Zealots

---

1. _____ a tax collector of ancient Rome, hated by Jews, usually rich, considered a sinner by Jews

2. _____ building used by Jews for worship; needed at least ten men to form one; found in villages; run by a rabbi or Pharisee

3. _____ annual Jewish holiday in memory of the escape of the Hebrews from Egypt; the holiday celebrated during the crucifixion

4. _____ the highest court of the ancient Jews; had 70 members; met near the Temple at Jerusalem

5. _____ building used for worship in Jerusalem; Holy of Holies housed at one time the Ten Commandments; priests sacrificed animals to atone for sins

6. _____ teacher of the Jewish laws

7. _____ member of one of the major religious parties of Jews; was in charge of the synagogue; very self-righteous and called a "hypocrite" by Jesus

8. _____ Greek word for "rock"

9. _____ a spokesman of God who taught God's will; one who saw into the future

10. _____ Greek word for "word"

11. _____ a fanatical, patriotic group of Jews who used violence to try and end Roman rule during Jesus' time; they were waiting for a Messiah who would be a king with an army.

12. _____ a group of men who lived in a commune near the Dead Sea and copied parts of Scripture; scholars think they are the group who may have written the Dead Sea Scrolls, which were found in 1947 near Qumran.

13. _____ Greek word for "defense attorney" or "Comforter"

BIBLE TEST

PART 2 — PEOPLE

a. Herod the Great
b. Elisabeth & Zacharias
c. John the Baptist
d. Jairus
e. Mary Magdalene

f. Lazarus
g. Nicodemus
h. Caiaphas
i. Joseph of Arimathaea
j. Mark

k. Paul
l. Pilate
m. Mary & Martha
n. Luke

---

1. _____ a Christian, Gentile physician who traveled with Paul; he was the author of a Gospel and the Acts of the Apostles.
2. _____ a king who wanted to kill the baby Jesus; he built major palaces throughout Israel.
3. _____ parents of John the Baptist
4. _____ ruler of a synagogue, a Pharisee who came to Jesus to heal his twelve-year-old daughter
5. _____ she was a woman from whom Jesus cast out seven devils
6. _____ Jesus' best friend, whom he raised from the dead
7. _____ sisters of Jesus' best friend, who attended to Jesus when he visited their home in Bethany
8. _____ took Jesus' body down from the cross and put it in his own tomb
9. _____ the Roman governor who agreed to crucify Jesus and then washed his hands of the whole incident
10. _____ a Pharisee who came to Jesus by night to ask questions
11. _____ a high priest of the Sanhedrin when Jesus was brought to trial in the Temple
12. _____ a preacher who lived in the wilderness and baptized people in preparation for the coming of the Messiah; the forerunner of the Messiah
13. _____ the apostle to the Gentiles in the early church; writer of several New Testament letters
14. _____ a scribe for Peter, one of Paul's fellow workers, writer of a Gospel

BIBLE TEST

PART 3

1. Name all twelve disciples:

a. _____   g. _____

b. _____   h. _____

c. _____   i. _____

d. _____   j. _____

e _____   k. _____

f. _____   l. _____

2. What does the Sermon on the Mount teach us about getting along with

people?

a. _____

b. _____

c. _____

3. Name five healings of Jesus:

a. _____

b. _____

c. _____

d. _____

e. _____

4. What did people in Jesus' time eat? _____

_____

_____

BIBLE TEST

PART 3 (Cont.)

5. Where did they find water? _____

_____

6. How did they light their houses? _____

7. What languages did they speak? _____

_____

8. Who ruled the country and people's lives? _____

   a. _____

   b. _____

   c. _____

9. Name the four Gospels: _____

   a. _____

   b. _____

   c. _____

   d. _____

10. How were women treated differently than men? _____

_____

_____

11. What was in the Holy of Holies in the Temple during Jesus' time? What

did the Holy of Holies represent? _____

_____

_____

BIBLE TEST

PART 3 (Cont.)

12. Name four qualities of Pharisee-type thinking:

    a. _____ c _____

    b. _____ d. _____

13. Tell what happened on each of these dates:

    a. 20 B.C. _____

    b. 8-6 B.C. (approx.) _____

    c. A.D. 27-30 (approx.) _____

    d. A.D. 70 _____

    e. A.D. 325 _____

14. In your own words, write a paragraph on what it means to be a disciple.

    _____

    _____

    _____

    _____

    _____

15. Explain the difference between Jesus' treatment of women and the Jews'

    concept of women. _____

    _____

    _____

    _____

    _____

BIBLE TEST
PART 3 (Cont.)

16. List six different Biblical names or titles for the Messiah or Christ.

    a. _____   d. _____

    b. _____   e. _____

    c. _____   f. _____

17. In your own words, describe Jesus' instruction on prayer.

_____

_____

_____

18. In your own words, how would you summarize Jesus' description of the

    kingdom of heaven? _____

_____

_____

_____

_____

_____

19. How does Jesus define his mission? _____

_____

_____

_____

_____

BIBLE TEST

PART 3 (Cont.)

20. Give three reasons why the Jews do not recognize Jesus as fulfillment of Old Testament prophecy. _____

_____

_____

_____

21. What is the significance of the walk to Emmaus?

_____

_____

_____

22. What does Jesus predict would happen after he is gone from the human scene? _____

_____

_____

_____

_____

23. After studying Jesus' life, what has had the greatest impact on your life?

_____

_____

_____

_____

_____

BIBLE MAP TEST

Directions: Copy the blank map on page 26. Find each of the following locations and write their names next to the appropriate dot on the map:

Cana	Sea of Galilee
Nazareth	Caesarea Philippi
Jordan River	Mt. Hermon
Emmaus	Territory of Decapolis
Bethlehem	Nain
Bethany	Sychar
Dead Sea	Tyre
Jerusalem	Sidon
Damascus	Caesarea Maritima
Territory of Samaria	Gergesa
Jericho	Mediterranean Sea
Capernaum	Territory of Judaea
Bethsaida	

CROSSWORD PUZZLE

ACROSS CLUES:
  2. another name for Matthew
  4. language spoken by most people in Palestine, including Jesus
  7. language of the Old Testament
  8. Jewish holiday celebrating Israel's deliverance from Egypt
  10. area in Palestine where Jesus spent the most time
  11. ten men could form this; Jewish worship was conducted here
  14. one of God's chosen people
  15. leather or papyrus book roll; the books of the Bible were in these
  16. earthly saying with heavenly meaning
  17. Jewish teacher
  18. language of the New Testament

DOWN CLUES:
  1. word meaning "Saviour"
  3. person from Samaria; Jews did not get along with them
  5. wise men who came to Jesus' birth and offered gifts
  6. enormous place in Jerusalem where animal sacrifice was offered
  9. weeds that grow side by side with wheat
  11. doctor of Jewish law; taught the law and copied it
  12. non-Jew
  13. person who speaks with divine inspiration
  16. tax collector hired by Romans

WORD LIST — BIBLE VOCABULARY:

Aramaic	Hebrew	Magi	prophet	Samaritan	synagogue
Galilee	Jew	Messiah	publican	scroll	tares
Gentile	Levi	Passover	rabbi	scribe	Temple
Greek		parable			

Copyright © 1993 by Kristy L. Christian and Kathryn L. Merrill

ANSWERS:

ACROSS:
2. Levi
4. Aramaic
7. Hebrew
8. Passover
10. Galilee
11. synagogue
14. Jew
15. scroll
16. parable
17. rabbi
18. Greek

DOWN:
1. Messiah
3. Samaritan
5. Magi
6. Temple
9. tares
11. scribe
12. Gentile
13. prophet
16. publican

GLOSSARY

Anna *(Luke 2:36-38)*
• A widow and prophetess (84 years old) who, together with Simeon, welcomes the child Jesus to the Temple. Luke tells us she "served God with fastings and prayers."

Antipas *(an'-ti-pas)*
• Son of Herod the Great, also called Herod the Tetrarch; a ruler of Galilee from 4 B.C. to A.D. 39 (Luke 3:1)
• Mentioned in the New Testament more than any other Herod
• Founded a city called "Tiberias," which was named for the Roman Emperor Tiberias
• Jesus called him "that fox" (Luke 13:31); when he heard certain Pharisees report Antipas' threat to kill him, Jesus referred to this ruler's evil permeating influence as "the leaven of Herod" (Mark 8:15).
• He illegally married his niece, Herodias (former wife of his half-brother). Herodias drew reproof from John the Baptist; John the Baptist condemned their marriage. After Salome (daughter of Herod Philip and Herodias) danced before Herod and gained from him the promise to grant her whatever she asked, Herodias instructed her to demand the head of John the Baptist (Matt. 14:1-12; Mark 6:17-29; Luke 3:19).
• In Luke 23:6-12, Pilate handed Jesus over to Antipas for trial because Jesus came from Galilee. Antipas treated Jesus with scorn and then handed him back to Pilate.

Antipater *(an-ti'-pa-ter)*
• Father of Herod the Great; Julius Caesar made Antipater procurator of Judaea in 47 B.C. He appointed Herod to be governor of Galilee.

Aramaic *(ar'-a-may-ik)*
• A group of Semitic dialects closely related to Hebrew; originally used by Aramaeans of Syria; in the New Testament: *Talitha cumi; Eloi, eloi, lama sabachthani* are Aramaic words; a dialect spoken by Jesus and his disciples was Galilean Aramaic.

GLOSSARY

Archelaus *(ar-ke-lay'-us) (Matthew 2:22)*
• Son of Herod the Great, who ruled Judaea 4 B.C. to A.D.6. When Mary and Joseph returned from Egypt and heard that Archelaus was ruler of Judaea, they decided to settle in Galilee.
• Very cruel to the Jews, so the Romans exiled him to France in A.D. 6.

Atonement
• Word means to be "at-one," reconciliation; Jews believed that for man and God to be reconciled sacrifice and offerings had to be made at the Temple; according to the New Testament, Jesus Christ came to reconcile man to God.

Caesar Augustus *(Luke 2:1)*
• Roman emperor from 27 B.C.-A.D. 14. He issued a decree for all the world to be taxed.

Caiaphas *(kay'-ya-fas)*
• The high priest of Jerusalem (A.D. 18-37); but Gospels have confusing accounts as to whether Annas or Caiaphas was a high priest.
• He is credited with influencing the Jews against Jesus with this statement, "... it is expedient for us that one man should die for the people and that the whole nation perish not" (John 11:49-50).
• During the trial, Jesus was brought from the residence of Annas to the palace of Caiaphas before being led to the Judgment Hall of Pilate.

Day of Atonement
• Yom Kippur. It was the only day of the year the high priest could go into the Holy of Holies. He offered a sacrifice for his own sin and the sin of the priests, then offered another sacrifice for the sin of the people. In the Holy of Holies, he sprinkled blood from the sacrifice. Then he took a goat, known as a "scape-goat," laid his hands on its head and sent it off into the desert as a sign that the people's sins had been taken away.

Elisabeth *(Luke 1:6)*
• Married the priest Zacharias; both described as having faultless characters
• She was barren — a tragedy for Jewish women. God gave her a child of great promise, John the Baptist, who was to prepare the way for the Messiah.
• Believed to be a relative of Mary, mother of Jesus

Essenes
- A devout group of Jews who lived in Qumran; monastic — celibate, disciplined, communal. Their purpose was to be ready for the final Day of Judgment. They copied manuscripts. They were wiped out in A.D. 70 after 200 years of existence. They hid their scrolls in caves near the Dead Sea. They were opposed to war; didn't believe in sacrifice; gave up worldly goods; read law of Moses day and night.

Gentile
- Non-Jew

Greek
- A spoken language for more than 3,000 years. The New Testament was originally written in Greek.

Hebrew
- Language of Old Testament with exception of small sections of Ezra, Jeremiah, and Daniel, which are in Aramaic

Herod, Agrippa I (*Acts 12*)
- King A.D. 41-44
- Grandson of Herod the Great, brother of Herodias; became ruler of Galilee, Samaria, Judaea. To please the Jews, he persecuted the Christians. He killed James, the son of Zebedee, and imprisoned Peter.
- Made king by Caligula

Herod the Great (*Luke 1:5, Matt. 2:1-19*)
- Ruler of Palestine from 37-4 B.C.
- Probably the Herod of Matt. 2:1, ruling at the time of Jesus' birth.
- Idumaean by birth but a Jew because his parents were Jewish converts
- After the death of his father and brother, Herod was given the title "king of the Jews" by the Roman Emperor Augustus. Herod finally captured Jerusalem in 37 B.C.
- He reconstructed the Temple which was begun about 20 or 19 B.C., it was not finished until A.D. 62 or 64. Jesus saw it develop but not finished.
- Had ten wives, five children
- Ordered death of all male infants in Bethlehem under two years old to annihilate every possible rival

- He rebuilt Caesarea Maritima. In cities he erected *stadia*, theaters, amphitheaters. Fortresses — Masada and Herodium — were built to protect him from his enemies. Masada was built for Herod to go to in case Cleopatra tried to take over his kingdom.
- 24 B.C. erected a royal palace in Jerusalem
- Vassal king — owed allegiance to Rome; free to run the kingdom as he saw fit but could easily be deposed and replaced by a Roman ruler or governor; foreign policy required Rome's approval. Romans placed friendly kings on thrones of countries that they conquered — "client kings." Herod was a buffer against Rome's enemies. Along the eastern Mediterranean sea coast, Rome established client states which could not back out of the agreement; the king was an ally.
- Life of King Herod was filled with intrigue, murder, and plots against his kingdom by his own family. He killed his first wife, Mariamne I; he killed Mariamne's mother. He named his son, Antipater, crown prince. Since two other sons — Alexander and Aristobulus — plotted against their father, Herod had them strangled. But then son Antipater tried to rush his father's death by ordering a fatal drug made. Antipater was arrested and tried before the Roman governor of Syria. He was put in prison.
- In Herod's madness, he locked notable Jews in the hippodrome. When he died, they were all to be killed. He also told his bodyguards to kill Antipater. Augustus in Rome is quoted as saying, "It is better to be Herod's pig than his son."
- Archelaus, son of his fourth wife, was to reign over the bulk of Herod's territory: Idumaea, Judaea, Samaria. Of the other sons, one, Herod Philip, was given Batanea and Trachonitis, and another son, Herod Antipas, became ruler of Galilee and Peraea. When riots started in Jerusalem during Passover, Archelaus called in the army and some 3,000 people were massacred. The Roman governor of Syria moved in to restore order. In A.D. 6 Augustus exiled Archelaus to France. From then on, a series of military prefects administered the province — the most famous was Pontius Pilate.

Herodias
- She was the granddaughter of Herod the Great who married two of her uncles — the first was Herod Philip. Then she left him for Herod Antipas. Angered at John the Baptist for denouncing this marriage, she influenced Antipas to behead John the Baptist.

Jairus *(jay'-i-rus)*
• The name may mean "he will awaken."
• Ruler of a synagogue in Capernaum whose dead daughter (twelve years old) was raised by Jesus (Mark 5:21-24, 35-43); in all three Gospels, the narrative is interrupted by a woman who had an issue of blood for twelve years.

Jew
• In the Old Testament, the Jews were members of the southern kingdom of Judah.
• Adherents of the worship of Yahweh as done at Jerusalem after the Exile. Soon the word referred to anyone who adhered to Judaism.
• In the New Testament, "Jew" refers to one who is Jewish by both nationality and religion.

John the Baptist
• Born about six months before Jesus; son of Elisabeth and Zacharias; thought to be related to Jesus because in all probability Mary and Elisabeth were cousins.
• In the wilderness, he fed on honey and locusts and wore coarse garments of camel's hair. He began his public ministry in the wilderness by proclaiming a baptism of repentance for the forgiveness of sins.
• He had disciples whom he taught to pray (Luke 11:1) and who fasted; some became followers of Jesus and carried John's messages to Jesus.
• Jesus was baptized of John in the River Jordan (Matt. 3:13; Mark 1:9; Luke 3:21).
• John's testimony of Jesus at the baptism was "Behold the Lamb of God . . ." (John 1:29).
• John the Baptist fulfilled Malachi's prophecy (3:1): "Behold I send my messenger before thy face, which shall prepare the way before thee."
• Jesus' strong endorsement of John (Matt. 11:11): ". . . there hath not risen a greater [prophet] than John the Baptist." Think how John the Baptist can be "more than a prophet" (Matt. 11:9).
• John's doubts as to whether Jesus is the Messiah when he is in prison: "Art thou he that should come . . .?" (Matt 11:3). Jesus responded by reciting the works as witness to his Messiahship.

Joseph
• Husband of Mary, mother of Jesus. He was of the house of David in

Bethlehem (Matt. 1:20); migrated to Nazareth where he was a carpenter.
• Pious Jew, observed the ordinances. When he discovered Mary's condition, considered breaking the engagement without publicity and any disgrace to Mary. Jewish custom said that engagement was almost like being married. She was sometimes called "wife." The woman could be dismissed from betrothal only by a letter of divorce. She was subject to the penalty concerning adultery. In Matthew's Gospel, the inference is that Joseph suspected her of adultery.
• Joseph is described as a just man (Matt. 1:19) and a devout servant of God. He was kind and wise.
• After learning the truth, he took Mary to Bethlehem to avoid any gossip, and for the census; took the family into Egypt for safety. It is presumed Joseph died before Jesus' public ministry.
• Gospel of Mark nowhere refers to Joseph
• Matthew pictures Joseph as receiving guidance from angels — the family fled into Egypt, returned from Egypt after Herod's death, then settled in Galilee instead of Judaea.

Joseph of Arimathaea (ar'-i-ma-thay-a)
• Member of the Sanhedrin, who buried the body of Jesus in a tomb on his own property. Matthew tells us he was rich, which is supported by the claim that he owned a tomb of his own — rock-hewn and unused. John tells us the tomb was located in a garden not far from the site of the crucifixion. "He took courage and went to Pilate and asked for the body of Jesus" (Mark 15:43). Luke hints that Joseph refused to give his consent to the action of the Sanhedrin in condemning Jesus (Luke 23:51).
• Joseph brought a linen shroud and laid the body of Jesus in a tomb and rolled a stone against the door.

Lazarus (laz'-a-rus)
• In Hebrew the word means "God has helped."
• Lazarus and his two sisters entertained Jesus and his company at their home in Bethany, on the shoulder of the Mount of Olives. Lazarus was taken ill while Jesus was in "retirement" east of the Jordan River. When Jesus did not come immediately after being called, Lazarus died, which Martha said would not have occurred if Jesus hadn't delayed. But when Jesus came, a great many witnesses were present at the tomb where Lazarus had lain four days already. The raising of Lazarus increased Jesus' popularity; it aroused

the antagonism of the Sanhedrin. This story appears only in the Gospel of John.
• Lazarus was also present at his home six days before the Passover at which his sister Mary anointed Jesus (John 11:1-44; 12:1-11).

Magi *(may'-ji)*
• Wise men from the East, could mean from Arabia, Mesopotamia, or beyond. Moffatt says "magicians." Goodspeed says "astrologers." They are not Hebrew; they are pagans.
• Jesus was accused of being a *magus* — casting out demons through Beelzebub.

Mary, Mother of James the Less and Joses
• She followed Jesus from Galilee, witnessed the crucifixion (Matt. 27:55; Mark 15:40; Luke 23:49), watched the burial, and visited the sepulchre on resurrection morning (Matt. 28:1). She was also designated wife of Cleophas, who was identical with Alphaeus — both names coming from the same Aramaic word.

Mary, Mother of Jesus
• ". . . a virgin shall be with child, and shall bring forth a son, and they shall call his name Emmanuel . . ." (Isa. 7:14; Matt. 1:23). Virgin birth only appears in the Gospels of Matthew and Luke.
• She and Joseph lived in Nazareth, but had to go to Bethlehem due to a census in their ancestral city. This has been challenged by many scholars, yet it fulfills the prophecy of Micah 5:2.
• Her sacrificial offering of two turtle doves at the Temple 40 days after Jesus' birth shows her and Joseph's economic status.
• The New Testament records the wise men from the East coming to see the child; the family journeyed into Egypt to avoid the persecution of Herod (the Great); settled in Nazareth upon their return.
• The New Testament narrates that once in Jesus' youth he was found in the Temple among the rabbis. Jesus knew his mission, but did his parents (Luke 2:48)?
• When Mary and Jesus' brethren sought Jesus (Mark 3:31), he defined his true relatives: those who do the will of God.
• Mary was at the foot of the cross when Jesus was crucified (John 19:25-27). While on the cross, Jesus entrusted the future care of his mother to the

beloved disciple, John. She is mentioned in Acts 1:14, where she and Jesus' brothers, together with the apostles, are pictured as participating in a prayer meeting following the Ascension.

• Qualities of Mary: deep spirituality, purity, faith, obedience to the divine will, trained her son in the religious traditions of his people; loyalty to Jesus.

Mary and Martha of Bethany

• Sisters of Lazarus (John 11:1; Luke 10:38)

• Mary served with her sister but was not distracted as Martha was. Mary sat at Jesus' feet and heard his word. Jesus commended Mary's wisdom in choosing to take the opportunity to hear Jesus rather than to help Martha with an elaborate meal (Luke 10:41). Martha complained that Mary was not helping her, but Jesus rebuked Martha.

• When Lazarus became ill, both sisters sent for Jesus (John 11:3). When Lazarus died, many Jews came to comfort them. Martha rushed out to meet Jesus, while Mary remained in the house. It is to Martha that Jesus said, "I am the resurrection and the life; he that believeth on me, though he were dead, yet shall he live . . . ."

Mary of Magdala (Magdalene)

• One of the most prominent of the Galilean women who followed Jesus

• Magdala was an important agricultural, fishing, shipbuilding, and trading center — a center of considerable wealth. Population was predominantly Gentile. It also had a hippodrome.

• We don't know when Jesus met Mary — Luke tells us that seven demons had gone out of her (Luke 8:2). There is no solid reason to believe she was a harlot. Joanna, wife of Herod's steward, traveled around with her in Galilee (Luke 8:1-3), and it is doubtful whether she would have traveled with a notorious courtesan.

• Mary helped Jesus in his Galilee mission and contributed financially to the venture (Luke 8:1-3); she went with him and his followers for his final appeal; she was present at the crucifixion (Mark 15:40; John 19:25); came to the tomb to anoint Jesus' body (Mark 16:1); reports the fact of the empty tomb and the message of the angels to the eleven disciples; was honored with a personal appearance by Jesus after the resurrection (John 20:11-18).

Moneychanger

• In New Testament times, a half-shekel offering in Tyrian silver coins was imposed by Scripture and had to be paid by every adult male.

• When pilgrims arrived from foreign countries for the festivities of Passover, moneychangers set up tables in the Temple court area to change foreign currency. They collected a fee for changing money.

• Jesus overthrew the tables of the moneychangers — those who were turning the Temple into a den of robbers (Mark 11:15; Matt. 21:12; John 2:14).

Nicodemus *(nik'-o-dee-mus)*

• A Pharisee and ruler of the Jews (John 3:1) and teacher as well — one who should have known the truth about God and His people. But the conversation Jesus had with Nicodemus showed he did not understand about the kingdom of God. He was a member of the Sanhedrin (John 7:50) and probably a very rich man. He visited Jesus by night, which indicates that Jewish leaders associated with Jesus only in secret. Yet, he sought a fuller understanding of Jesus' meaning.

• He also undertook a legalistic defense of Jesus against the Pharisees because they had not heard firsthand what Jesus taught. He displayed a real concern for Jesus in the face of the hostility of his friends.

• Final mention of Nicodemus is in John 19:39, where it says he helped Joseph of Arimathaea in preparing the body of Jesus for burial. He provided a huge amount of spices to be placed between the folds of the linen cloth in which the body of Jesus was wrapped for burial — but even this was carried out in secrecy for fear of the Jews.

Oral Tradition

• *The Interpreter's Dictionary of the Bible* offers the following information: "Tradition is the foundation of culture, a spiritual bond between the present and the past, between the individual and the greater fellowship in space and time, of which he is an integrated member. What man knows, his experiences and insights, what he has felt and thought and expressed in words, has, as far as it has been deemed important for the life and welfare of the community, been handed down by the tradition of mouth and example. This means also in rather fixed forms, but nevertheless always gradually and unconsciously adapted to the changing circumstances and interests of the changing ages. Man's memory of the past and his religious ideas and usages make no exception" (Vol. 4, p. 683).

• Who handed down the tradition? People who were especially concerned with the life and interests in question — elders, the judges of tribal communities, priests, prophets, scribes of court and temple, professional story-tellers. In certain areas where accuracy was very important, tradition had to be learned by heart.

• Tradition lasts as long as interest in it survives. Without interest, it will die. The narrative must appeal to the emotions of the audience and it must be exciting.

• A genuine tradition has its basis in something "real," — an actual event, a locality, a sociological and political relation. But it can also have its origin in "some learned theory or speculation of later times." In Palestine one hears a lot from guides who say today, "Tradition says . . . ."

• For the Jews, the Mishna (a commentary on Old Testament texts) and the Talmud were orally transmitted for centuries. In the synagogue, it was long forbidden to say the Torah from a written scroll.

• Talmud: The conviction was that ". . . besides the written Torah (Law) — the Bible — there had been from the first, from the divine communications to Moses at Sinai . . . an oral Torah, handed down from generation to generation, which lawgiver and prophets strove to engrave on the hearts of the people. As teacher succeeded teacher in synagogue and school, their teachings and often conflicting opinions, all based on the Bible, were treasured. Through long practice the power of memorizing had been greatly strengthened, but the accumulated mass of oral traditions and teachings became so unwieldy that the best memory could not be trusted" (*The Interpreter's Dictionary of the Bible*, Vol. 4, p. 511). So the need arose for a compilation which would summarize the most essential teachings and preserve for future generations this wisdom. Thus the Talmud was produced. It ranks second only to Hebrew scriptures.

• ". . . The oral law serves to transform the Torah from a mere written document, liable to become obsolete, into a continuous revelation keeping pace with the ages" (op. cit., p. 512).

• "The fundamental, conscious transition from oral transmission to script is done when critical outer and/or inner circumstances threaten to break off the living tradition" (op. cit., p. 685). It happened to Israel in 586 B.C. — captivity in Babylon. It was impossible to save books. The archives in Jerusalem were destroyed. In exile, the remnant had to write down the old traditions so that connections with their spiritual foundations would not be severed.

Papyrus
• Tall aquatic reed plant. At one time, abundant in lower Egypt. Thin strips of the inner pith of the papyrus stalk laid vertically, with another layer placed horizontally on top. An adhesive was used and pressure applied to bond them together into a sheet. After drying, it was polished with shell or stone implements; then the sheets were glued together to form rolls.

Parable
• In Hebrew the word means "to set side-by-side." In Greek it means "a placing beside, a comparison."
• Earthly saying with heavenly meaning; a brief narrative for didactic purposes. Jesus used it to teach what the kingdom of heaven is and what is specifically required of people for entrance into the kingdom. Parables clarify what obedience to God means and how that obedience effects our relationships with others.
• They reflect the character of Jesus' good news — his summons to repentance.
• Hearers find themselves listening to familiar examples of everyday life where the words Jesus speaks are so simple and clear that a child can understand and translate them into external life lessons.
• Approximately 39 parables given in the Gospels

Passover
• Celebration of Israel's deliverance from Egypt
• Refers to whole range of observances during the season
• Pilgrim festival — as many as 100,000 may have come to Jerusalem annually for the feast
• Passover eve involved ritual slaughter of the sheep and goats at the Temple with sacrificial sprinkling of the blood against the altar, and later that night a domestic meal which symbolizes the role of fellowship and historic observance.
• Sometime between noon and 3:00 p.m., slaughtering of the Passover sacrifices began at the Temple, announced by a trumpet blast sounded by the Levites. Priests tossed the blood against the great altar and burned the portions of fat on the altar — symbolizing the releasing of the redeeming action of God for His whole people. Legs of the animal were not to be broken. Each animal was given back to the family and roasted in a clay oven. People dressed in festive white. A lamb was eaten with bitter herbs. The question is asked, "Why is this night different from all other nights?" Thus the song and

story begins.

• Passover is far more than an annual commemoration of remembering the Exodus. In every generation a man is to regard himself as if he had gone forth from Egypt just as his ancestors had done.

Pompey

• In 63 B.C., Pompey, a Roman general, captured Jerusalem, and Judaea became a puppet state of Rome. In 55 B.C., Pompey, along with Crassus and Julius Caesar, controlled part of the Roman Empire. After Crassus' death, a conflict arose between Caesar and Pompey. Pompey was defeated; he fled to Egypt where he was later assassinated.

Pontius Pilate (pon'-shus pi'-lat)

• Fifth Roman procurator or governor of Judaea, Samaria, and Idumaea (A.D. 26-36). His headquarters were at Caesarea Maritima, but he came to Jerusalem during the major festivals like the Passover because the influx of visitors gave rise to disorders. He brought imperial images in violation of Jewish laws against use of such images; he used soldiers to stop disorders among his subjects.

• The night council of priests and elders sent Jesus to Pilate the governor, since only the Roman representative could sentence people to death. Pilate gave Jesus the opportunity to deny the charges that he perverted the nation and would not give tribute to Caesar; Jesus was silent. Pilate wondered (Mark 15:5) and asked, "Art thou King of the Jews?" (Luke 23:3). Jesus answered, "Thou sayest it."

• Pilate told the multitude he found no fault in this man — he admitted Jesus' innocence (Mark 15:14). The people again accused Jesus of stirring up the crowds with his teaching. Pilate then sent Jesus to Herod, but Herod returned him to Pilate.

• Pilate tried Jesus in the Praetorium which is a part of the Tower of Antonia in the ancient Temple area. Pilate's wife warned him, "Have thou nothing to do with that just man." Fearing the multitude stirred up by the high priest, Pilate pronounced the sentence of death. Pilate washed his hands of the whole affair and delivered Jesus to be crucified.

• Some of the original pavement where he displayed Jesus to the people has been found under the Church of the Dames de Zion. Soldiers had scratched games on the pavement as they waited during the trial, and those marks can still be seen today.

• Pilate appropriated Temple funds to build an aqueduct to bring water to Jerusalem from the Pools of Solomon near Bethlehem.

• Pilate slaughtered a number of Samaritans who searched on Mt. Gerizim for the golden vessels reportedly hidden there by Moses. Rome sent for him to stand trial for this blunder.

Pontius Pilate's Wife *(Matthew 27:19)*

• During the trial of Jesus, Pilate's wife sent a message to him saying, "Have thou nothing to do with that just man: for I have suffered many things this day in a dream because of him." The opportunity was given Pilate to avoid crucifying Jesus.

Publican

• Tax collectors hired by Romans to collect various taxes

• They collected tolls on the borders of countries and cities, at bridges, landing stages; collected tolls from those transporting property (including slaves) by land or sea.

• Jews hated tax collectors. Many felt that any act of submission to Caesar — such as paying a tax — was treason to God. It was felt that Jews who did this work were despicable because publicans sold their services to a foreign oppressor and engaged in literal robbery against their own people.

• In the New Testament, they were classified with sinners and prostitutes.

• Luke 19:2-10: A Jew — Zacchaeus — was a chief tax collector. Jesus was a guest in his home.

• Matthew was a tax collector.

Sacrifice

• This involved the slaughter or burning of an animal; an offering did not. Bones were not to be broken.

• The Old Testament claimed that man could find forgiveness from God through sacrifice, which supposedly removed the effects of sin. It was believed that God was alienated by man's sin and required something to appease His anger before He would again show favor to the sinner.

• Jesus was called the "Lamb of God" in the New Testament, and a lamb was used for sacrifice.

Salome *(Mark 15:40)*

• One of the women who followed Jesus from Galilee. She was with other women at the cross. They bought sweet spices for anointing the body of Jesus and when they arrived at the tomb, they discovered it was empty.

Salome
• Daughter of Herodias and Herod Philip; during the birthday celebration of Herod Antipas (and at her mother's request), she had the head of John the Baptist brought to her on a platter.

Samaritan
• Originally, inhabitants of Samaria — the capital of the Northern Kingdom of Israel
• When Assyrians conquered the ten northern tribes in 722 B.C., many Jews were deported. So foreigners were imported to replace them. Intermarriages occurred with those left behind — consequently a mixed race of Jews and foreigners from Mesopotamia and Syria called "Samaritans" came into being.
• Samaritans believe Gerizim alone will escape the destruction of all things. Scholars do not know the date, but a separate temple on Mount Gerizim was built. It was destroyed in 128 B.C. They did not accept the Temple in Jerusalem as the place of worship and sacrifice.
• They accepted only the first five books of Moses as Scripture and authentic Law of God. To them, Moses was the exalted prophet, the seal of the prophets, the apostle *par excellence*, choicest of creatures, utterly a unique being. The whole world was created for his sake.
• Strict observance of sabbath — no one allowed to stir from his house except to attend services.
• In Jesus' day — bitter hostility between Samaritans and Jews. Jews from Galilee passed through the hilly country of Samaria in order to reach Jerusalem as it was the shortest route.

Scribes *(Matt. 13:52; 9:3; Mark 9:11, 14; 12:28)*
• Most were Pharisees, their legal opinion became part of oral tradition.
• Doctors of the Law, copyists, editors, guardians of the textual purity of Scripture; in the New Testament, teachers of the Law, lawyers, or rabbis. Their main objective was to preserve the legal system built into the text of the Law. They lectured on the Law in synagogues, debated it, and applied it in judgment.
• They were not paid for interpreting the Law; had to have another profession.
• Some belonged to the sect of the Pharisees; also associated with chief

priests and elders. Apart from chief priests and members of patrician families, the scribe was the only person who could enter the supreme court — the Sanhedrin. Pharisaic party in the Sanhedrin was composed entirely of scribes (like Nicodemus).

• Scribes from Jerusalem interrogated Jesus by challenging him on points of the Law.

• What gave power to the scribes? Knowledge of Scripture. A scribe had the right to be called rabbi, though others who had not gone through the regular course of education for ordination were also called rabbi.

• Scribes were the guardians of tradition, but also believed to have secret knowledge attributed to divine inspiration. (Apocalyptic writings of late Judaism contained esoteric teaching of the scribes.) Nicodemus came to Jesus by night to receive from him the teaching on the innermost mysteries of the kingdom of God, of regeneration and redemption.

• 1st century A.D. — they were against spreading the Aramaic translation of the Old Testament.

• Thought of as successors of the prophets. Their words were believed to have sovereign authority; reverential awe and unbounded respect was poured on them. In a synagogue, the scribe had the seat of honor.

Scroll
• Leather or papyrus book roll. It could be up to one foot wide and 30 feet long. If it was long enough, it was fastened to a stick or wooden pin, around which it could be rolled and unrolled for reading; found in every synagogue. Jesus read from a scroll of Isaiah in the synagogue at Nazareth.

Simeon (Luke 2:25-35)
• A "just and devout" man, waiting for the "consolation of Israel." He welcomed the child Jesus into the Temple. He also foresaw Jesus' mission: "A light to lighten the Gentiles, and the glory of thy people Israel." He predicted the difficult mission which awaited Jesus.

Stephen
• First Christian martyr (Acts 6:5). He was appointed to distribute food and other necessities to the poor in the growing Christian community in Jerusalem. This gave more time to the Apostles in the ministry.

• Stephen also taught and preached in the synagogues. Many who were jealous of Stephen's wisdom trumped up a charge that he was speaking blasphemously against Moses, so the Jewish elders had him brought before the Sanhedrin. False witnesses accused him of saying that Jesus would destroy the holy place of Jerusalem and change the customs which Moses delivered.

• A mob seized him and stoned him to death at a place adjacent to the city wall, which may be near to the present Stephen's Gate in the Eastern wall. Saul, later Paul, witnessed the stoning.

• His martyrdom touched off persecutions which scattered the Christian community.

Synagogue

• Probably first erected during Babylonian captivity (6th century B.C.) when the Jews no longer had the Temple in Jerusalem in which to pray and teach.

• Means "congregation" or "assembly"

• By A.D. 70, 480 synagogues in Jerusalem. Each one consisted of a house for reading the Law and a place where schoolchildren received their primary instruction. All synagogues were destroyed when Rome destroyed the Temple in Jerusalem.

• Service on the sabbath consisted of readings from the Bible (one from the Law and one from the Prophets). Services always began with the *Shema*: "Hear, O Israel, the Lord our God is one Lord; and thou shalt love the Lord thy God with all thine heart, and with thy soul, and with all thy might" (Deut. 6:4). Always read in Hebrew, but most Jews during Jesus' time spoke Aramaic, so an interpreter gave a verse-by-verse explanation (a *targum*).

• Furnishings included a Torah shrine where one or more Torah scrolls and probably some prophets' scrolls were kept. It was a chest (sometimes called "ark") and covered and screened from the sight of the congregation with a veil or curtain. In the center was the *bema*, or elevated podium, for reading of the lessons and benedictions.

• People sat on stone benches, not chairs, along the walls. Women and children sat in a separate gallery from the men upstairs.

• A menorah or seven-branched candlestick or lampstand was located in the large assembly room.

• Open three times a day for prayer

• Torah was read through once in three years.

• It was customary to invite any stranger who happened to attend the services to deliver a prophetical lesson.

• At least ten elders were required to form a synagogue. They also chose a

head of the synagogue.
• No animal sacrifices, no altar

Temple
• Symbolic dwelling place for God
• Only place where animal sacrifices occurred
• In 20 B.C., Herod the Great started a renovation which lasted until A.D. 64 (John 2:20); Herod's Temple was destroyed by Rome in A.D. 70. The Dome of the Rock, a Muslim shrine, now occupies the site.
• The Temple Mount area contained a large courtyard and several inner courts. Debates and teachings occurred in the Court of the Women or the Court of Gentiles — here large crowds would gather.
• The moneychangers put their tables in the Court of Gentiles.
• Solomon's Porch was along the eastern side of the Temple Mount area.
• The Temple contained the Holy Place and Holy of Holies; a veil separated the two areas. The Holy of Holies could only be entered by a high priest once a year. In Old Testament times, the Holy of Holies contained the Ten Commandments.
• Inside the Court of Priests was the bronze laver for cleansing purposes and the altar of animal sacrifice.
• The table of shewbread, the seven-branched candlestick, and the altar of incense were located in the sacred precincts of the Holy Place.
• In Jesus' time, the Holy of Holies contained no furnishings.

Tiberius *(Luke 3:1)*
• Roman emperor from A.D. 14-37. He was the adopted son and successor of Augustus. According to Luke, it was in the fifteenth year of his reign (27 or 28) that John the Baptist began his preaching and Jesus began his ministry.

Zacharias *(zak'-ah-ri-as)*
• Father of John the Baptist (Luke 1:5-67)
• Righteous priest; burning incense was his duty at the Temple. While performing this task, an angel appeared to him and announced that his desire for a son would be fulfilled.
• His son, John the Baptist, would be filled with the Holy Spirit and prepare the people for God's rule. Zacharias asked for a sign — he was stricken with dumbness for his unbelief until the promise was fulfilled. When John was circumcised, Zacharias, a deaf-mute, amazed his friends and family by

confirming his wife's unusual choice for a name, writing on a table, "His name is John." Then Zacharias was again able to speak; he blessed God and was filled with the Holy Spirit. He then prophesied the fulfillment of Israel's Messianic hope.

Zealot
• Fanatical patriots who believed in the coming of a David-like king as Messiah; wanted Jewish independence from Rome
• Willing to fight to the death (guerrilla fighters)
• Simon the Zealot was a disciple. Barabbas might have been a Zealot.

BIBLIOGRAPHY

A Commentary on the Bible, ed. Arthur S. Peake. New York: Thomas Nelson & Sons, 1919.

Barnes, Albert. *Barnes' Notes on the New Testament.* Grand Rapids, MI: Kregel Publications, 1962.

Berrett, LaMar C. *Discovering the World of the Bible.* Provo, UT: Brigham Young University Press, 1974.

Bright, John. *A History of Israel.* Philadelphia: Westminster Press, 1959.

_____. *The Kingdom of God.* Nashville, TN: Abingdon Press: 1953.

Bruce, F. F. *New Testament History.* New York: Doubleday, 1971.

Burrows, Millar. *What Mean These Stones?* New York: Meridian Books, 1957.

Charlesworth, James H. *Jesus Within Judaism.* New York: Doubleday, 1988.

Clement of Alexandria. *The Rich Man's Salvation,* trans. G. W. Butterworth. Cambridge, MA: Harvard University Press, 1982.

Cornfield, Gaalyah and David Noel Freedman. *Archaeology of the Bible: Book By Book.* Peabody, MA: Hendrickson, 1976.

Dodd, C. H. *About the Gospels.* Cambridge, England: Cambridge University Press, 1950.

_____. *The Bible Today.* Cambridge, England: Cambridge University Press, 1968.

_____. *The Founder of Christianity.* New York: Macmillan, 1970.

Dummelow, J. R. *A Commentary on the Holy Bible.* New York: The Macmillan Company, 1908.

Durant, Will. *The Story of Civilization,* Part III, *Caesar and Christ.* New York: Simon & Schuster, 1972.

Edersheim, Alfred. *Sketches of Jewish Social Life in the Days of Christ.* Boston: Ira Bradley & Co., 1876.

_____. *The Life and Times of Jesus the Messiah.* Massachusetts: Hendrickson Publishers, 1883 (recently reprinted).

_____. *The Temple, Its Ministry and Services as They Were at the Time of Jesus Christ.* Grand Rapids, MI: Wm. B. Eerdmans Publishing Co., reprinted 1990.

Eusebius. *Ecclesiastical History,* trans. Kirsopp Lake. Cambridge, MA: Harvard University Press, 1980.

Finegan, Jack. *Archaeology of the New Testament.* Princeton, NJ: Princeton University Press, 1969.

_____. *Light From the Ancient Past,* Vols. I & II. Princeton, NJ: Princeton University Press, 1959.

Grant, Michael. *The Twelve Caesars.* New York: Charles Scribner's Sons, 1975.

Great Events of Bible Times. Garden City, NY: Doubleday, 1987.

Great People of the Bible and How They Lived, ed. G. Ernest Wright. Pleasantville, NY: Reader's Digest, 1974.

Hastings, James. *Dictionary of the Bible.* New York: Charles Scribner's Sons, 1909.

House, H. Wayne. *Chronological and Background Charts of the New Testament.* Grand Rapids, MI: Zondervan, 1981.

Jeremias, Joachim. *Jerusalem in the Time of Jesus.* Philadelphia: Fortress Press, 1969.

_____. *The Eucharistic Words of Jesus.* London: SCM Press, 1966.

_____. *The Parables of Jesus.* 2nd ed. rev. New York: Charles Scribner's Sons, 1972.

_____. *The Prayers of Jesus.* Philadelphia: Fortress Press, 1978.

_____. *The Sermon on the Mount.* Philadelphia: Fortress Press, 1963.

Jerusalem Revealed: Archaeology in the Holy City 1968-1975, ed. Yigael Yadin. Israel: The Israel Exploration Society in cooperation with Shikmona Publishing Co., 1975.

Jesus and His Times, ed. Kaari Ward. Pleasantville, NY: Reader's Digest, 1987.

Keller, Dr. Werner. *The Bible as History*. New York: William Morrow, 1956.

Keyes, Nelson Beecher. *Reader's Digest Story of the Bible World*. Pleasantville, NY: Reader's Digest, 1962.

Latourette, Kenneth Scott. *A History of Christianity*, Vol. I, *Beginnings to 1500*. New York: Harper & Row, 1975.

Manson, T. W. *The Servant Messiah*. Grand Rapids, MI: Baker Book House, 1977.

Millard, Alan. *Treasures from Bible Times*. England: Lion Publishing, 1985.

Miller, J. Lane and Madeline S. *Harper's Bible Dictionary*. New York: Harper & Row, 1961.

Moffatt, James. *The Bible, A New Translation*. New York: Harper & Row, 1935.

Odelain, O. and R. Séguineau. *Dictionary of Proper Names and Places in the Bible*. New York: Doubleday, 1981.

Pax, Wolfgang E. *In the Footsteps of Jesus*. New York: Leon Amiel, Publisher, 1976.

Pearlman, Moshe. *Digging Up the Bible*. New York: William Morrow and Co., 1980.

Sergio, Lisa. *Jesus and Woman*. McLean, VA: EPM Publications, 1975.

Shotwell, Berenice. *Getting Better Acquainted with Your Bible*. Maine: Shadwold Press, 1972.

Smith, William. *A Dictionary of the Bible*, ed. F. N. and M. A. Peloubet. Nashville, TN: Thomas Nelson Publishers, revised 1986.

Stagg, Evelyn and Frank. *Woman in the World of Jesus*. Philadelphia: Westminster Press, 1978.

Strong, James. *Exhaustive Bible Concordance*. Grand Rapids, MI: Baker Book House, reprinted 1981.

Sundemo, Herbert. *Revell's Dictionary of Bible Times*. New Jersey: Fleming H. Revell Co., 1979.

Swidler, Leonard. *Biblical Affirmations of Woman*. Philadelphia: Westminster Press, 1979.

Teringo, J. Robert. *The Land and People Jesus Knew*. Minneapolis: Bethany

BIBLIOGRAPHY

House Publishers, 1985.

Thayer, Joseph H. *Thayer's Greek-English Lexicon of the New Testament*. Grand Rapids, MI: Baker Book House, 1977.

The Anchor Bible, Vols. 29 & 29A, ed. William Foxwell Albright and David Noel Freedman. Garden City, NY: Doubleday, 1970.

The Anchor Bible Dictionary, ed. David Noel Freedman. New York: Doubleday, 1992.

The Gospel According to Thomas, trans. A. Guillaumont. New York: Harper & Row, 1959.

The Holy Bible, King James Version. England: Cambridge University Press, [no date available].

The Interpreter's Dictionary of the Bible, Vols. 1-5. Nashville, TN: Abingdon Press, 1990.

The Lion Encyclopedia of the Bible, ed. Pat Alexander. England: Lion Publishing, 1986.

The New English Bible with the Apocrypha, ed. Samuel Sandmel. New York: Oxford University Press, 1976.

The Revised English Bible. England: Oxford University Press, Cambridge University Press, 1989.

The Works of Josephus, trans. William Whiston. Peabody, MA: Hendrickson Publishers, 1987.

Thompson, J. A. *Handbook of Life in Bible Times*. England: Intervarsity Press, 1986.

_____. *The Bible and Archaeology*. Grand Rapids, MI: Eerdmans Publishing Co., 1962

Twenty-six Translations of the New Testament, ed. Curtis Vaughn, Th.D. Grand Rapids, MI: Zondervan Publishing House, 1967.

Where Jesus Walked, ed. William H. Stephens. Nashville, TN: Broadman Press, 1981.

Wilkinson, John. *Jerusalem As Jesus Knew It*. London: Thames and Hudson, Ltd., 1978.

Wilson, Ian. *Jesus: The Evidence*. New York: Harper & Row, 1988.

Witherington, Ben, III. *Women and the Genesis Of Christianity*. England: Cambridge University Press, 1992.

Yamauchi, Edin. *Harper's World of the New Testament*. New York: Harper & Row, 1981.

— CHILDREN'S BOOKS —

Atlas of Bible Lands, ed. Harry Thomas Frank. New Jersey: Hammond, 1984.

Barclay, William. *Jesus of Nazareth — The Easter Message*. Cleveland: William Collins & Sons, 1978.

Connolly, Peter. *Living in the Time of Jesus of Nazareth*. London: Oxford University Press, 1983.

Doney, Meryl. *The Man Who Changed History*. England: Lion Publishing, 1988.

Dowley, Tim. *Jesus and the Big Picnic*. Chicago: Moody Press, 1987.

Miley, Barbara. *Biblical Archaeology For Teens — Discovering Everyday Life in Bible Times*. San Diego: Rainbow Publishers, 1988.

Schultz, Lorraine. *Biblical Archaeology For Teens — Discovering Jerusalem*. San Diego: Rainbow Publishers, 1988.

_____. *Biblical Archaeology for Teens — Discovering the New Testament*. San Diego: Rainbow Publishers, 1988.

Smith, Barbara. *Young People's Bible Dictionary*. Philadelphia: Westminster Press, 1965.